Michigan's Er

An Anthol

Compiled and Edited by
Z Publishing House

2018

Table of Contents

Foreword, or How This Series Came to Be

There is a troubling catch-22 that exists in the world of publishing: in order to be published—at least by any of the major houses—you must already have been published. The logic works like this: Publishing houses want to sell books. What easier way to sell books than by publishing authors who already have amassed large followings of readers to whom they can market? Inevitably, this cycle leaves the aspiring author with the pressing question of where to begin. Sure, the dramatic rise of self-publishing platforms has enabled everyone to put their writing out there, which is great, but it does come with its own set of problems. Namely, when everyone actually does put their writing out there, as has happened, the question now becomes: Where are the *readers* to begin? With the oversaturation of the market, readers could spend entire lifetimes buying and reading self-published books and still not find that one author with whom they truly resonate. On Amazon alone, for instance, a new book is uploaded every five minutes, and that number is only set to rise as more and more people take advantage of the self-empowering platforms available to writers today.

The good news is that readers want to discover new talent. This we learned firsthand after beginning Z Publishing in November of 2015. What started as a small Facebook group designed to bring independent writers together on a shared platform of exposure soon transcended into a wave of newfound appreciation for independent writing. Within a few short months, Z Publishing had amassed tens of thousands of followers across social media. Once we knew the idea had struck a chord with a growing group of people, we took the next step and launched Z Publishing's own website in March of 2016. Publishing articles from writers of a multitude of genres—including travel, fiction, politics, lifestyle, and poetry—the website garnered more support from readers and writers alike, and our following continued to grow.

Furthering upon our mission to promote the work of talented wordsmiths across the nation, we began a series called America's Best Emerging Poets, through which we showcased our favorite up-and-coming poets on a state-by-state basis. After the success of our first series, we decided to open submissions to prose writers as well. Thus began our Emerging Writers series, a collection of short writings from a wide variety of genres—including literary fiction, mystery, and narrative nonfiction—through which we hope to offer our readers a quick and efficient way to discover new local talent and perhaps entirely new genres that otherwise may have been too daunting to explore.

While working on this series, and as our base of physical retailers has expanded, we've also been able to take perhaps the most significant step forward in our publishing evolution, and we now proudly offer solo-author book deals. To make the selections on who to offer these deals to, we will take into account reader reviews, so if there are any writings within this book that you particularly enjoy, be sure to give them a mention in your Amazon review!

Now that you know a bit about how this series came to be, we'd like to thank you for taking the time to explore this edition of the Emerging Writers series. We hope you enjoy this publication, and we look forward to hearing your thoughts regarding how, together, we can build the publishing house of the future.

-The Z Publishing Team

The Disappearance of Hannah Sinclair
Bryce Meerhaeghe

At twelve years old, Hannah knew her father was not a good man. They trudged through the forest behind their house, the bitter cold and snapping twigs making the shadows seem even more fearsome to the young girl. She held her jacket close to her chest, focusing on the man walking before her. He paused from time to time to hold back branches for her, but these brief moments were an exception; she may as well be walking through the woods alone, the silence between father and daughter only amplifying the crackling of the brush beneath their feet.

"I'm cold," she tried, no longer taking the silence. Her father replied with a small grunt.

The throbbing in Hannah's calves told her they must've walked for miles before finally arriving at a small clearing in the forest: a patch of blackened grass and cut trees giving way to the sky above. Hannah stared, transfixed by the view of the cosmos. Far from the lights of her suburb, billions of stars could be seen high above, pinpricks in the dark blue ocean of the universe with nebulas adding splashes of pink and green to the mix. Hannah's heart fluttered for a moment, choosing to believe that her father brought her out here, a night where the New Moon would not obstruct this view, to relish in the stars she dreamed of visiting one day. She could almost picture it, smiling at the blue marble she once called home as she floated in a space shuttle high above the atmosphere.

"Mhmm!" Marshal's throat clearing brought her back to Earth, her heart sinking even further when she saw what he was gesturing to. With an outstretched hand, Marshal Sinclair pointed to a strange altar in the center of the clearing. It was made from the only tree stump that appeared to have remained unharmed in the fire that formed the clearing, surrounded by three fox skulls polished white in stark contrast with the ground. The skulls were connected by loose trails of small bones that circled the stump, an eclectic array of ribs, femurs, and spinal columns that all appeared to be from different animals. Sticking out of the stump itself, three wooden spikes made from tree branches rose in line with the skulls, as if they were guideposts for their placement. Hannah gulped, fearing what came next.

"I need you to help me finish it," Marshal said, his cold monotone revealing nothing. Hannah shook her head, her eyes never leaving the spikes.

"Hannah, inspect the altar."

She shook her head again, her heart beating faster against her ribs.

"Hannah, do you love Daddy?"

Hannah looked at him, feeling her eyes sting. There was no warmth in her father's expression, yet no hint of malice either. His face remained slack, devoid of emotion as if he were stating the obvious. As she nodded, she could feel a few tears run down her cheeks.

"Inspect the altar." For a moment, Marshal's eyes became a little glossier but he wiped the evidence away, returning to his vacant face as if nothing had cracked. Hannah turned back to the altar, her body shaking from her silent sobs and fear. She could feel her own muscles fight against her, her legs attempting to lock up and stop their progression, but Hannah slowly marched on. She was only a foot from the altar when she felt the hands against her back. She fell the remaining distance and landed on her stomach. She retched out a choked scream, blood pooling quickly beneath her as well as across her back, staining the white t-shirt she wore as well as her blue sweatpants. She attempted to rise from the spikes, but the wood grinding against her raw flesh sent shockwaves of pain through every nerve. Her heart raced against her punctured chest as tears mixed with the blood on her face.

She jumped as she felt a hand gingerly touch her cheek. She looked up to see the tear-stained face of her father, gently holding her face and using his thumb to wipe away her tears. In the back of her dying mind, she knew she should spit blood in his face, the face of her killer. *At her sixth birthday, her father was filming her as she blew out the candles of a rectangular cake with chocolate frosting.* She fought back the memory. *She smiled to the camera as her mother wrapped the young girl in her arms, kissing her on the cheek as her friends applauded her achievement; she did blow out all the candles, after all.* She looked up into his eyes; he stroked her brown hair. *With cake in hand, she leaped from the blue picnic table and attempted, to ambush her friend, who saw her coming and was quick to throw her cake preemptively. Hannah dodged and threw her cake, missing her target and hitting her father in the stomach. He fell over in a mock scream, twitching from time to time in the grass as he heard his wife's stifled laughter. Hannah ran to her father's side, shaking him gently to play along but never holding back her smile. Before she could even react, Marshal quickly scooped the cake off his shirt and pushed it gently into his daughter's face, knocking her to the ground. He scrambled to his feet to flee, leaving the camera in the grass as Hannah gave chase.*

The Confession of Ferdinand Michelle
Kyle Mykietiuk

Working with seniors, you hear a lot of strange things. But let's not mince words, I was working with the dying. Ferdinand Michelle was one of them. He didn't do much, drank a lot, read some . . . He was dying from liver failure I think. One night, very late, he spoke to me. This was his last confession.

"I was never able to find the music in life. There was a time, in my youth, when I picked up the meager harmonics of that seemingly unblemished song, but it soon faded away from me, and I was never able to hear those frequencies again. I tried my best to follow those precepts, of Aristotle, Russell, Wittgenstein—my fellow colleagues of scientists and philosophers— but every time I heard the whisperings of rationality in my ears, every time I inclined myself to listen to its voice permeating through my head, every time I acted on its instinct, behaved on its behalf, believed in its capacity to enhance my life, I was always met with calamity in the end. I always miscalculated, always misstepped, and at the end of each day I was always met with the most stifling revelation of all—that I was bored, that I was acting as a machine, a slave to the external stimulus that I plugged into my brain, a slave to reason, that I had lived life in accordance with a perspective of which I had no experience, and with that came a blind obedience that proved detrimental to me. Maybe I was trying to live someone else's life, always pumping my brain full of ideas which originated out of histories that were much different than mine. I had lived as a ghost, haunted by systems of thought, rules and codes that did nothing for me, that only made me miserable the more I tried to grope around and grasp something tangible in that cold darkness, and if logic could be transmuted into matter, it would be cold and dark. Make no mistake about it! They would turn it into bullets, in order that we might be able to kill ourselves with them . . . or kill each other! That's all it's good for in the end! Just look around! Where has it gotten humankind?"

At this point I start to pick up on some sort of aggravation in his voice, like he's being inflicted by some sort of mysterious, cabalistic pain. He raises his inflections, his face gets red. He really starts bellowing it out. You can hear the hurt in his tone, the modulations of his voice extending and regressing, seemingly uncontrollably, a mad dog barking in the wind.

"His universal religion, his objective language? What benefit has his bondage to that over-glorified bitch provided him? He has worshiped reason since he was first able to comprehend his insipid thoughts, since he was first able to utilize information and compute it through his over compacted noggin . . . yes! Since the first things of consciousness could be picked at and scratched, he's scratched! He's never stopped scratching! Bleeding, raw, scabbed and scarred over! Doesn't matter! He's never stopped! He never will!

Well, what has it done? Tell me! I defy you to answer! Has it brought him prosperity? Utopia? Opulence and security? No! Nothing! Nothing but the contrapositive! Oh, my dear friend, look around! It has betrayed him, forsaken him! Left him with cities, careers, money, debt, wars, pollution, poverty . . . what misfortune has it abstained him from? The macro to the micro? Nothing! Traffic, drugs, starvation, murder! It has buried humankind and it will be his undoing and his extinction. He is too conscious of it, and that, my friend, is a sickness of which there is no cure, a disease which will debilitate him, and in the end, he will grow sick of it and he will kill himself. Future's curtain will part and it will reveal nothing, every second which passes is a precursor to it . . . every breath waiting in harmonious unison, waiting eagerly in anticipation for the big show! And every second after—well, it's harder to say—after we finally know the score, I don't think there will be enough love left to go around, not enough that will be able to sustain life . . . and a loveless world is a dead world, a world without seconds, or minutes, or hours, or days."

"But make no mistake, the stage is being set amidst this cosmologic whirlwind, set smack dab in the center of the void! Absolutely nothing! A black hole without light, without love, without anything meaningful! Barred of all purpose! The Earth! The decomposing organ of a rotting God, a God whose limbs and viscera lay splattered across the dark and empty canvas of the entire nugatory universe! Suns, moons, comets, planets! It's all the festering and bloated flesh of a God who mutilated himself under the compression of his own pointlessness! All his logic, all his reasoning, the "laws of nature" . . . well here he lies! Behold the spectacle! First row seats to the funeral, the ceremony . . . as active participants no less! Look what it's done him, all his logic! What a laugh!"

"What are we then? If God is dead and rotting in this cosmic tomb, what becomes of us? Simple! The maggots! The maggots feasting and gnawing off his fermenting flesh! The byproducts of a mistake, an error, a suicide that stemmed from too much understanding, too much logic! The first premise was made in error. We've flourished in error! But through this error we've discovered a truth, an eternal and paramount truth, a truth which is about to be made apparent to all the peoples of the Earth, and when the curtains drop we'll be slack-jawed, bewildered and shocked by this unforeseen swindle from our venerated destiny! This creative twist! We'll hang our heads, downcast and disheveled, depressed, and more importantly, unamused . . . after the credits roll there will be nothing else for us to do other than bite down on the barrel of a gun and pull the trigger . . . collectively, hand in hand, side by side . . . an entire race cashing in its chips after losing so much . . . for millennia upon millennia, century after century of getting suckered into a raw deal . . . a stacked deck, weighted dice. We've lost it all, now we're bankrupt. So what else is there we can do? Give up the ghost, I say, and I think that after knowing what it's all been for we won't make a fuss about it! And so for that reason, I drink! I forget reality, I throw it away, I disregard my self-respect, I become an insect! The maggot that I am! I embrace error, I revel in contradiction!"

He died the next day. No one ever came to visit him. He is buried somewhere—I'm not sure where, I don't think anyone does. Nobody understood, neither did he.

Diagonally
M. Andrew Bodinger

The apartment's elevator serviced twenty stories of residents, who on their daily exodus compacted together without even offering one another an acknowledged, horizontal smile. But it was midnight when Lavinia led Solomon into that complex, and the only hint of the morning rush was the elevator's textured floor, trampled with dozens of muddy shoeprints. Solomon's Beijing dormitory employed an over-night staff who washed the floors and watered the elevator to purify all but the deepest-rooted filth. He learned that night that Beijing apartments were not afforded the same luxury as the towering dorms of international students at his temporary university.

The pair undid their hands as the doors fretted and collapsed in hesitant synchronicity. Lavinia stood with one hand resting on her hip and the other anchored by her purse. She adjusted her skirt, feigning aloofness as she stole sly glances at Solomon. Her stomach was alleviated of her alcohol-induced ache as if it was a fog that blew away in the smoggy wind. Solomon peered at the elevator doors, using the refracted light as a mirror. He guided his fingers to break-up the hair clumped by sweaty adhesive and pretended he didn't notice the near-stranger admiring him. The near-stranger who wrapped her arm around his and whose head was slumped on his shoulder for the length of a cab ride.

The elevator quivered with mechanical coughs as it climbed. Solomon usually counted the seconds by fidgeting with whatever token he uncovered in his pockets but didn't want to flip his dying phone on or count the remaining cash in his emaciated wallet. Instead, he cracked his neck and tensed and untensed his muscles. When the doors unclenched to evict them from their bubble, Lavinia stepped out and extended her arm, while at the same moment Solomon's hand made another pass through his hair. They snickered and smiled at the unmet gesture, and she grabbed his forearm to slip her hand into his.

"Don't touch the walls," she said, motioning to the rough, white corridor. They passed over the unmopped tiles and around a corner, their steps no longer in sync as Solomon inched behind her. Solomon had been to a few dim holes in the wall over his stay in China, but those were walk-ups near to campus. He wondered if drug addicts were pitching themselves under Chinese decorative knots or if hallways were just undervalued in a cosmopolitan city. He stopped walking for a moment and gathered strength to tell her he was going to turn around, when she spoke again and pulled him along. "Don't touch anything, just to be safe."

Under the club's searchlights that night, Lavinia had asked Solomon if he would accompany her back to her humble flat. This was the first time he had clearly heard her voice. *She has an English accent* he thought. The whole night they shouted over the music between dances and sips from their shared mojitos. A former journalism major and Hong Kong native that traveled between home and Shanghai most of her life *who is interning with a human rights lawyer in Beijing.* She even studied in America for a year and they traded pictures of Chicago's museum fronts and skyline. *Why should you feel embarrassed? She picked you as her dancing partner, friendo, she picked you.*

With a stream of "um's" and half-finished questions, he settled with a "Wait, really?" Enamored by the uncertain facial expressions he construed as his eyes struggled to process her suggestion. She grabbed his hand and left the club, a chain named Elements, to wave for taxis in the street and to haggle with black cabs idling on the curb. The question why would only hinder the momentum.

As they waved and called to the passing drivers, Lavinia's eyes fluttered shut and her weight increasingly pushed on his. By the time someone pulled over, they resembled less of a couple, and more like a skiving opportunist carrying a blacked-out woman. But she maintained a rhythm as she walked; her first step to scout out the uneven, gray tiles, and the following two extended in succession as Solomon hazarded one measured step to keep pace. In this pattern, before sliding into a cab and after crawling out, they made it to her apartment.

Once inside, her clomping heels charged forward and strung Solomon beside a lucky red door emblazoned with the golden numbers "1705." She looked back at Solomon with a mischievous grin that flattened as she dug through the intertwined mass. She almost overturned the purse between her embarrassed scoffs before unhinging her ring of keys from a pair of knotted Apple earbuds.

"Home sweet home," she said. Her lilt was vibrant and convincing, one that silenced him again and lulled him through the threshold. I am in her home. This should be the edge of elation. A knot of earbuds that will inevitably untangle.

Solomon wasn't one to get in others' way. He apologized for other people bumping into him and paid for spilled drinks he was nowhere near. But when her advances became too obvious to miss and she led him through the Salsa, he didn't care who he cut through on the crowded dance floor. After they left and her mojitos tranquilized her, time set in. He had left his friend Arvid behind.

"Public transportation is pretty good in this city," he had told Arvid once, "And cheap too—for us, anyway. Why bother standing in the road like an idiot to hail a taxi?" After his initial trip from the airport, Solomon swore them off and disparaged their use for the entirety of his time in Beijing and passionately vetoed their suggestion when going out. And yet, when Lavinia invited him, he wordlessly followed her lead. For all he knew, the driver was in cahoots with Lavinia to steal his passport and kidney, and he was just thankful for the compliment. Arvid brought him to Elements in the first place, and Solomon left him with nothing but a limp wave as he helped Lavinia into their taxi. *I am a selfish wandering snob. This should be worth ditching your friends for though, right? I should be happy. Aren't you supposed to grab her butt and make-out at the club? Grind to a mash-up of popular songs, pretend the world was always a blur?* At least, he later recalled, she used her phone's app to pay for the ride and spared him the indignity.

Her apartment was a step-up from the corridor. The walls and ceiling were still a musty white, yet she and her roommates' wooden floor had a crisp sheen. Lavinia flipped a switch that illuminated the kitchen and the living area into just above an ambient shadow reflecting off the slick-looking floors.

A head resting on the arm of the old couch rose with the lights. "*Salut,* Lavinia," a man said. Solomon later realized that his teeth were chattering, likely because he was only in his boxers and the apartment was a good ten-to-fifteen degrees colder than it outside.

"*Ça va,* Benjamin?" Lavinia asked, initiating a brief chat that lasted until she guided Solomon into her narrow bedroom.

"You speak French?" he asked. *Is that the only thing on your mind, man?*

"English and Mandarin and Cantonese from birth, French in high school. Some Korean." She dropped her purse amidst picture frames and a charging Mac on her wooden desk. A dozen pairs of shoes lined the wall. Her bedspread was a turquoise design with the words "Your Text Here" sprawled in a fluffy font. Half of her space was a separate room where she hung her clothes, towels, intimates on intricate metal drying racks.

"Five whole languages?" *And she picked me.* "When do you have time to sleep?" He joked with a breathy laugh.

She smirked and sat on the bed. "Here and there." Solomon stood for a while, limp, letting himself sway and glanced around her room looking for nothing in particular, as if he were standing on the Eiffel tower looking for icebergs. "Take a seat." She patted her sheets. An invitation. He hesitated, at first pretending not to hear her, and when he did sit down, he did so a body apart. She scooted and closed the gap and placed her hand on his knee, exchanging with him half-smiles as she and her face tilted closer to him.

Solomon's body shook. He concentrated on stiffening his muscles to a dull rumble and was barely cognizant of their kiss.

"Are you nervous?" she asked. Their kissing at the club, however middling, was far superior to this trembling statue.

"Just cold I think."

"Want me to turn the heat on?"

"It's still summer. Don't worry about me."

"No, you're my guest. Just give me a second." She sprang off her bed and into the living room. Solomon heard mirthful French in the distance.

14

After she cleared the room, Solomon opened his wallet. *55 kuai. Enough for a cab? Possibly. What part of the city are we in? No way to know. Phone is dead, or near dead. Effectively dead,* he decided. On the cab ride over, she handed him her phone with her address plugged in to the GPS so he could follow the cab's route, but the street names and directions were in unfamiliar characters. Her phone's recommended route was the same the driver took incidentally, and Solomon was so impressed that he pushed away any concerns that the isolated highway was a direct path from Beijing's party district, *Sanlitun,* to China's friend and buffer, Pyongyang.

He fell back onto the bed. After several moments he rolled onto his side then hopped with his leg and shoulder over to the corner facing the wall. He closed his eyes and laid his head back into his forearm.

The flow of blood in his arm slowed but he supposed that if he could focus, sleep would come in spite of it. *Any minute now and I'll reset.* Lavinia rounded back into the room. Solomon listened carefully. He could hear her gaze as she balanced herself on the wall and kicked off her heels. When she noticed the lump in on the corner, his heart flared. She considered it before hitting the light and crawling next to it.

"Solomoooon," Lavinia said, as if coaxing a ghost, and turned quiet. She whispered into his ear.

"Hey there, sleepyhead. You're alone again, just like at that shitty club. Mind if I join you?"

She doesn't have an accent when she whispers like that. Her voice must have retreated when she went to turn on the heat and is still speaking French to the naked man on her couch, leaving her body with nothing to articulate except a hoarse, humid cloud. Solomon didn't move anything, not a finger, not even his eyes under his lids. Every minute or so Lavinia would adjust her weight on the bed, her limbs encroached more tightly around the brick sinking into the mattress. A sleepy brick, one that only moved to take slight breathes through its nose, and to let his heart pound feeling back to his forearm.

Lavinia whined. A cute glottal sound that burrows into spines. Solomon focused on stilling his shaking body when she whined again, louder and longer. His chest spiked. Pretend to be asleep. She whispered into his ear but he didn't understand it over the beat of his heart and her burning breath. He flipped over, all at once, and kissed her forehead to satiate her, but kept his eyes shut and held her arm and torso with non-committed grips.

They kissed again. Her lips tasted like the distinction between cold and moist. *I'm asleep!* He wanted to tell her. *I'm asleep, and I do not dream of you.* She whined once more, taking ambivalence as a challenge. He leaned further to stretch his tongue into her mouth like an olive branch. Not deeply, just enough for a faint ebb and flow.

He gave in more and more; held her arm, kissed more abrasively, let her taste his ear. But never opening his eyes. She reached her hands into his pants and he felt her dimpled grin through their pressed foreheads, as her arm traveled down and down, and then up again and again, as if reaching to knock on a closed red door. Solomon's mouth retracted and his forehead tensed reflexively. Quivers, attached to whatever bulge traveled through his chest, traveled up and down with her hands. Then, it kept going up. It lurched up through his stomach, tunneled through his esophagus, and splattered the back of his throat.

"Where is your bathroom?" he asked with a gurgle. He dashed out of bed, one hand over his mouth and the other pulling his pants up. He was half-way out the door when he heard the mumble of the word 'left.' Before going far into the living room the bathroom, he spotted the bathroom on his left. *Thank God it's right here.*

He plowed his face into the toilet and emptied the night from his stomach as a few short, stringy globs. It didn't last long even with a few extra heaves. When the episode ended he leaned against the wall, lacking the energy to even flush. The back of his head and shirt may have been sprinkled with the walls white specks, he realized, but he focused on huffing and buttoning his pants.

"What happened?" she asked, standing in the door frame. She found her accent again. This was the first time that he saw her clearly, and he forgot what she sounded like. Even after a night dancing in a club and fooling around in bed, she seemed put together. Her hair rested on her shoulders as if conserving its energy, her eyes unbending in neither playfulness nor seriousness. In the doorway she projected herself with strong, model-like stance, and her height, whether it was short or tall, became an unmeasurable abstraction.

"I had too much to drink." A lie, they both knew. He had sobered up the moment they climbed into the cab.

"Did I do something wrong?"

"It's not you." Solomon zipped his jeans.

"Why did you dance with me or go home with me if you didn't like me?"

"It's . . . not you."

"You said that. I want a real answer."

"You're perfect. I wanted to go where you wanted to go. Why did you pick me?"

"You were the first person I noticed. You seemed like somebody I—"

"Thanks. I appreciate it. But right now I just don't want to be here. Or anywhere else, to be honest." His words tasted like acid. "I like your name, by the way, it suits you. I wish I wasn't so afraid to say it more tonight."

"It's not my real name, I hope you know. It's a name I chose when I first went to an international school."

"I learned something today and I'm sorry that I had to ruin your night in order to learn it. But I know now that I can't t be nobody and be nowhere at the same time." He didn't know what else to say, and, feeling uneasy, he poured his face back into the toilet and closed his eyes. His phlegmy vomit flailed in its death throes. He rested in its radiated heat. She didn't leave for another minute, but he felt her gaze leave him for the distant architecture of her bathroom. She looked up at the water stains in the ceiling or the drip in the shower hose over the toilet, things she never would have noticed had she something to say or someone to say it to. When she returned to her room, her steps no longer clomped but were a rambling shuffle against the wooden floor.

He got up and peeked through her door; she was covered by her duvet in the darkness He shut it and retreated to the living room. Luckily, Lavinia neglected to lock the front door, so he wouldn't have to feel bad about leaving her door unlocked.

"*Au Revoir, pengyou.*" The voice on the couch chattered in both languages. Solomon waved without turning around.

The brown steps on the floor shifted, Solomon thought, as the elevator crawled down the shaft. The choreography of the rain walkers was now in a different alignment below him, each step moved to form a pattern more easily followed. He exited the elevator and strode out of the apartments and through the courtyard of overgrown, gray tiles. He didn't walk with conviction. Instead, kept his furtive hands in his pockets as he left through the front gates.

As he stepped out of the premises, a cab turned a corner and perused the empty street. He reached for its attention with broad extension.

"Beijing Language University," he said in broken Chinese through the cracked window.

"Gotcha," the driver probably said.

Solomon watched the driver as he sat in the back seat atop the wicker seat cushion. The industrial jungle of apartments with barred awnings and clothes hanging between the bars wasn't new or exotic anymore. Beijing was a city with a late bedtime and an early start. The in between was unmemorable compared to any given taxi-driver. Arvid told him about a driver he met once who inquired about his nationality. After answering, the driver greeted him with an off-hand Swedish phrase he learned from a middle-eastern classmate in college. Anyone who memorizes a city ought to be interesting and an adroit judge of character, Solomon figured, but his driver just smoked through the crack in his smudged window.

The heads of the front seats had screens implanted into them that silently played the same loop of skincare and hair ads. The women in the commercials had skin that was as pale as Lavinia's. As pale as his. The driver wasn't a taxi driver his whole life, Solomon deduced, whose skin was dark and cracked, like the skin of the cleaners in the streets who picked up trash and cigarette butts with long, wooden tongs. Solomon worked pool construction most summers before, and even if college didn't prepare him for a suit-and-tie

17

job for the rest of his life, he would always be as pale as the Chinese women in these ads.

"How much will this be?" Solomon tried to ask.

"No more than it needs to be," he probably said. Solomon nodded.

"Listen," he probably said, "forget today. It is not suitable for you to regret it. Go home and sleep on your bed diagonally. Tomorrow, get up early and study."

"*Xie xie,*" he said and nodded again. The driver craned his neck, clicked his tongue and shrugged.

They arrived at the university gates. The number on the machine was 33 *kuai.* Solomon handed him two twenties and left, not waiting for change. The black barred gates were just ajar enough for him to strafe through. He found his dorm, one of two adjacent towers of international students. He walked ten flights of stairs, tiptoed passed his sleeping roommate, and sat in bed. He stretched his legs out, the only light a dim streetlamp cutting through the gap in the curtains and elucidating the edge of his sheets only half-attached to the mattress. If one of the students in the opposite dorm had a long eyeglass and spied through Solomon's window, all they would see were the limbs of a single vignette parsed by ruffled sheets.

Those of the Red
Eli T. Mond

Walking in a single file line were eight figures, all hidden under robes as red as roses thriving in their prime. The land, far-flung and barren, was shrouded in a primordial darkness, lit by nothing more than a full, yet distant moon. The robed figures moved in absolute silence, their motions barely disrupting the dust-covered earth. It was as if they weren't sovereign beings unto themselves and were merely the shadows of something truly tangible.

They trekked on through the night until they finally arrived at their destination—the peak of a life forsaken hill. And as they reached the Earthen Acropolis, they formed a circle around a stone cube that, upon first inspection, seemed to grow from the soil itself, on account of the crooked roots bursting from its sides. The object was no more than six feet in all its dimensions, and most of its moss infested surfaces bore no remarkable features, save for a curious array of seemingly connected images carved into its topmost side.

At the center of the mural was a woman, full-bellied and with a halo of eight interlocking circles emanating from Her head. The graciousness of Her aura suggested she possessed a royal, perhaps even a divine, status. Her legs were agape, showcasing Her feminine anatomy, and placed between Her thighs was a cube. And beneath the cube was a weeping eye with a dagger plunged medially into the iris. The punctured eye was surrounded by eight, bowl-like indentations, equal in both depth and the space between them.

The arms of the birthing Woman reached up towards an Ouroboros, and on each side of the creature were two, vaguely humanoid, beings. The one on the left stood with its right hand raised, while the one on the right stood with its left hand raised; and each hand held a vine that formed an arch over the serpent and entwined at the point of contact.

The soft, white light of the moon caused the carvings to emit a faint glow, compelling the figures to disrobe and stand completely bare against the midnight air. Among them were four men and four women standing in an alternating order, all with skin blacker than the vacuum of space, making them almost invisible against the nocturnal backdrop. The only things that effectively distinguished them from the night were their glassy, silver eyes that burned like sixteen peculiar stars.

One by one, each of the naked figures approached the cubical altar and held out their left index finger, from which a drop of an oily black substance fell into one of the eight indentations surrounding the punctured eye. Once they were finished, they all reassumed their positions in the circle and watched as the cube was swallowed into the ground.

Once the object was entirely hidden from their sight, they directed their attention to the moon. And as they gazed upon the pale form, its usual palette of whites and grays turned a deep red, as if some alien battle had coated the surface in a sea of blood. From that, now crimson, body poured a mist of the same color that seemed to simultaneously exist in an aqueous and gaseous state. The skin clad disciples fell to their knees and planted their faces in the dirt, averting their eyes from the blinding display.

As the mist descended through the firmament, a thunderous sound was heard and the heavens receded like a scroll into the horizon. From the beacon of red light, a wispy apparition as tall as the highest mountain appeared with its arms outstretched. Its breath was that of a tempest, and its eyes were that of the primordial fires from which the multiverse was forged.

It was a magnificent, yet ominous spectacle, capable of driving the strongest soul to the awe-inspiring edge of mortal sanity. However, despite its magnitude, only a small number of individuals throughout the world were actually capable of seeing the manifestation. And those whose eyes were touched by the ancient spirit felt no fear, for they knew they were to be spared the agony to come.

Strangers
Jared Sebastian

Sweat behind your knees, loud chirruping air in the afternoons, broad green wherever you look. The breathing, breathable swamp. The flat gray streets, wide sidewalks. The sun's fingers laying on the brown rooftops. I saw it scurry under the counter.

For two weeks every summer my parents sent me to Florida to stay with Papa and Meemaw. Papa was short and stubby like a toe, and red all over. Meemaw was tall and thin with wiry red hair, almost as red as Papa's skin. Papa and Meemaw were my mother's parents. My mother was old, so I knew my Papa and Meemaw were very old. My Papa and Meemaw lived on Crestfall Lane in Jacksonville.

Down the street was the high school where Meemaw told us she went when she was a girl, where they have the tennis courts where me and Katie could go and play tennis when Meemaw would tell us to go on and get out the house. Katie is my cousin, and she would come and stay with me when I went down to Florida. Katie's family lived in Florida, and Katie was always tan and wore short shorts and tank tops, and she never got bothered by getting sweaty or when bugs would fly in her hair.

Katie loved to play and go on adventures, like when we found that ditch with the big cement pipe where the water ran out, and we threw things inside of it and screamed. Katie was never afraid to talk to the older kids who sometimes came around the high school. Katie always wanted to be outside, and I liked to stay in and read in front of a fan, but I liked Katie because sometimes she would say we could stay inside and she would lay on the couch and let me read to her while she closed her eyes and imagined the pictures the words were making up, and sometimes we'd switch and Katie would read to me and stand behind the fan and do funny voices.

Papa and Meemaw had a nice house that wasn't very big but it was bigger than my mom and dad's, and it had a room called a sunroom where all the windows had screens in them, where my Meemaw kept her plants, and sometimes on really rainy days when it seemed like it would just be raining forever me and Katie would sit there by the window and listen to the thunder and wait for raindrops to flick our noses. There were lots and lots of pictures of my mother and Papa and Meemaw's family on all of the walls in their house and sitting on Papa's piano he never played.

My last summer in Florida was when I was thirteen and Katie was fifteen and in high school. We spent the days that summer usually riding bikes or playing tennis at the school or badminton in the backyard or asking Meemaw to take us to the mall, or sometimes I read and Katie listened like we used to, but Katie had a phone then so we didn't do that very often. At night though we couldn't play around, because Papa was sick and we had to be quiet. My parents told me about it before I went down, but I didn't really understand it until I was there in the house.

During the day, my Papa told us cheesy jokes and showed us card tricks, but at night Meemaw told us we had to stay in our room and just go right to sleep because Papa would get confused and angry. So that summer at night, we stayed in our room and we listened to Papa's heavy feet banging here and there around the house. Sometimes we'd hear the TV hum to life and the voices that came out would be turned up earsplittingly loud, and it would sound like Papa was talking back to the people in the shows or on the news. Sometimes the TV would just be turned on and then a minute later it'd be shut off. The fridge would wheeze open, plates would clatter. Sometimes he would start yelling for Meemaw, and he called her by her name, Kathy. She'd come out of her room sounding sleepy, and she'd tell him to quiet down, and sometimes they'd start fighting. That summer listening took the place of telling stories to each other at night.

It was like Papa became a different person after the sun went down. We awaited the arrival of this stranger into the house every night, with the blanket wrapped around our shoulders and the flashlight held between us. Katie was in high school so she tried to be mature about it, which meant she wouldn't laugh with me when I laughed at Papa's hollering, so quickly I learned to stop laughing. I don't think we knew ourselves why we stayed up so late and listened so intently. I think maybe it just would've seemed foolish to ignore it.

A couple of times we heard glass break. Sometimes he'd start calling my mother's name, or my aunt's name, asking Meemaw where they were or when they would be home. Or sometimes he called other names we didn't know. One night he knocked on our door, which startled us. The sound of my heart beating sounded too loud. Meemaw told him my mother was sleeping in the room, and she got him to sit down when she told him she'd make him a sandwich. The night after that she told us we had to start locking the door before bed.

If the nights were strange, then the days were even stranger. Often Papa would sleep in late, and when he awoke there'd be a lot of sleep in his eye and he always asked Meemaw for some coffee in a scratchy voice, but after he read his paper and drank his coffee, it was like he remembered I and Katie were there all of a sudden, and he was thrilled to see us. Then he was just Papa again, the one we knew. He talked in silly voices and repeated the news headlines to us, always looking over at us for a laugh as we ate breakfast, and I think it was his look more than his silly voice that always got us laughing. Some afternoons he'd make us his honey and banana sandwiches and sing his country songs with loud bravado in the kitchen as he sliced the bananas. But all of this happiness was so strange in light of the tense nights where the stranger roamed free. I wasn't sure how to feel about it, but I knew

22

something wasn't right. It kind of felt like my heart was moving around inside of me and couldn't find a place to land, not feeling safe particularly anywhere. A peculiar longing to go home to my mother and father would hit me sometimes out of the blue.

Very quickly Katie and I noticed that Meemaw was not acting like herself, either, but in a less frightening, quiet way. As a kid, you become very skilled at spotting when adults are trying hard to be happy. It's almost a psychic thing, really, because it has nothing to do with what you see or hear, nothing to do with your brain at all, like when you just know that someone behind you has got their eye fixed on you. Katie started to play less with me as the days went by, and spent more time with Meemaw helping her clean around the house or cook dinner, or sometimes they just sat at the table and talked. I was glad that Katie was there to do that, because I wasn't sure I could say anything to Meemaw at all. She was sad in a way I didn't understand, at least just then. She and Papa would talk to each other for our sakes, but it was like they were being gentle around each other in a way that was unnatural. When she would come in to kiss us goodnight, though, I made sure each time to give her a big hug, and she always liked that, I think.

On one of our last days there, we woke up at the same time, very very early in the morning, when the sun had just barely cracked the sky, turning it a gentle dark blue. Katie said it'd be fun to sneak into the kitchen and eat some of the Rocky Road ice cream Meemaw had bought us the night before, and it made me nervous but I was hungry and oddly enough ice cream did sound good.

The whole time going about it we couldn't dare to look at each other for more than a split second or we'd be close to bursting with laughter. We'd got the bowls and spoons and ice cream and scooper out when I saw the cockroach skitter across the wood-panel kitchen floor. I jumped and cupped my hand over my mouth and that made Katie jump and flip her bowl and she looking down where I was looking but she didn't scream and her eyes just got really big. The cockroach had stopped right on the floor between Katie and I. It just sat there, menacing, slick and dark brown and oily, those hair-like antennae moving rapidly, scanning, reaching, feeling. I stepped away slowly, wanting so desperately to have my naked feet a million miles away from this place. Katie reached over the counter in a flash and grabbed Meemaw's wide shining butcher knife.

What? I mouthed to her.

She looked at me and responded only with a desperate look in her eye, and I knew that she felt as naked as I did. She held the knife tight and steady, and for the life of me I could not imagine what she was planning on doing with it, but then the cockroach moved and we both screamed in unison, and Katie dropped the large knife and its edge hit the cockroach, severing its back end from the rest of it, and all of this happened in slow motion.

23

Down the hall, a door opened and then slammed against a wall, but I hardly noticed as I was caught up in staring at the cockroach, wobbling and leaving a trail of something behind it I couldn't imagine, its remaining legs carrying it wildly to the small inch beneath the cabinets. Then Katie grabbed my arm and pulled roughly, and I looked up and saw my Papa there in the kitchen looking at us with a startled expression, and I knew then that he did not recognize us.

"What are you doing in here? What are you doing in my kitchen?" he yelled. "Who are you? Who are you?!"

Then Papa charged at us and Katie pulled me again, and I swung around and we ran out the front door, my Papa close at our heels. He came down the steps and chased us across the yard, and out the front door behind him came Meemaw in her nightgown, yelling my Papa's name and telling him to come inside. We ran out into the street and Papa followed us. I looked back once and I saw an ugly look in his eye, the first time I'd ever seen such a look before, some ugly feeling was in him that I didn't know people could have towards other people. He cursed at us, using words I knew he wasn't used to, calling us "little thieving bitches." We got to the corner when Meemaw caught him and got up in his face and started pulling him towards her, saying his name and her name over and over, through her weeping. I saw some neighbors come to their porches. Papa had stopped so we stopped too.

I looked at Katie and she had a tear going down her face, and I felt tears rolling behind my eyes too. There was a lot of energy in me, like an engine kicking and roaring, and I felt like I should run, and I also felt shaky and weak. I felt the strange sensation of having been ripped so suddenly from a familiar place and feeling into something unfamiliar, kind of like on a roller coaster that shoots you into a dark tunnel when it first jets off and it takes your mind quite a minute to catch up. A real sadness was catching up with me then, as I watched my Papa's face settle back to its natural state, kinder and more childlike, the face I knew, the one I sat across from playing checkers and eating lunch. Then I saw my Papa's face get very red, as my Meemaw explained who Katie and I were. He began to nod his head very slowly up and down, like he was being scolded by someone we couldn't hear, and I saw him get redder and redder till he choked up, and he began to cry.

I watched Papa squat down and then sit on his rear end, and he cried like a little child into his hands. He kept saying "I just lost my head, I'm sorry. I'm sorry, girls." Meemaw waved us over and Papa took both our hands as he sat there on the sidewalk and I felt how warm and worn and fragile his hand was, and he continued weeping and saying he was sorry, and I wanted for him so badly to stop, and instead we all wept there together in our bare feet.

In Case of Fire, Use Stairway
Halley Bass

You shatter through the glass and feel the pieces claw into your skin and shred. Your blood is free from its confines, it seeps over your eyes and up your sleeves and gives you a copper mouth, your nerves pinpoint every splintered shard and protest their intrusion and your feet have broken the air.

You ponder the curvature of the Earth and the hazed white and blue that you see through the dripping red. You're nearly in space and you wonder how you can breathe until you realize you really can't. Your throat is dry and your mouth is dry and your tongue is dry and black with ash and you look away from the stubbornly blue sky, the haze grows gray.

The wind presses as if to push you higher, blisters your skin and roars in your ears and you wonder if this is so different from burning? Is it better? You had a choice.

If you were burning, there would be less glass embedded under your fingernails.

If you were burning, hazed white and blue would be lucid orange, white, yellow flame caressing wooden door frames. Your feet would rest on heat-cracked linoleum instead of searching through surfaceless air.

You think of him because he pulled glass out of your finger once, held your hand as the remnants of your dinnerware lay strewn across the floor. He smiled at your clumsiness and you smiled too because not returning a smile from him is impossible. You remember you couldn't help but squirm.

Just hold still, it'll be over in a moment. You did, because you trusted him. You do it now because your limbs feel stiff and numb in the charred air anyway and you still trust him.

You think of him because you like it more than thinking about the other thing, the gray haze is closer, closer, closer it develops into solid ground, and you remember standing in your bedroom naked, unsure of what to wear. He told you the place was formal and you could tell this was a special occasion because you don't do formal. Black tie dry and black with ash closer, closer, closer is beyond both of your budgets. Your head fills with images of golden wedding bands and champagne and you didn't think he'd ask like that but maybe he'd been watching too many movies on that new television he got for Christmas.

He might watch this, too.

It will be on the news—

You were unsure of what to wear standing in your bedroom naked and you supposed work clothes would have to do the windows in your office blew out and your coworkers screamed and then he called to you from the bottom of the stairs.

Are you coming, dear? Our reservation is for five. The meeting with your project manager who lay sprawled across his desk with rebar through his throat is at fi—

Yes, I'm coming down.

Coming down.

Coming down.

You think of him again but it doesn't really matter what you think anymore because the concrete gets the last word.

Him and Her
Leah Blaetterlein

The blanket was itchy on her bare skin. The sheets that smelled like Downy had been kicked off the bed the night before and the spare blanket was the only thing that covered her bare body. She rolled to her right and propped herself up on one arm. The alarm clock on the bedside table read 8:47 AM. She let herself fall back onto the bed and curled up in a ball, pulling the multi-colored wool blanket up over her shoulders. She closed her eyes and pulled the blanket up to block out the early morning sun that seeped in through the half-closed curtains. Her mind this morning was consumed by guilt. There was only one person she wanted to see, and it wasn't the person she had sex with last night. She quickly sat up and threw the blanket off. Her clothes were strewn all over the room: her shirt by the door, her pants some feet from the shirt, and finally her bra and underwear by the bed. She quickly got off the bed, now embarrassed that this was the situation she was in. She got dressed and grabbed what little stuff she had with her. There was no point in waking the person who lay sleeping in the bed. She didn't remember his name anyways.

Rose was beautiful, even if she didn't think so. Every time he saw her, he became more infatuated with how beautiful she was, and how she effortlessly lit up the room. He always studied her closely, noting every little change in her appearance from the last time. Her blonde hair fell just above her shoulders, her natural hair color becoming more apparent as it began to show on the top of her head. She had bright blue eyes that were sometimes gray, which also had a hint of green in them sometimes. He thought the color changed depending on the day. Her nose had freckles on it, and it seemed like they were perfectly sprinkled across it, some of them landing on her cheeks. She had a contagious smile that was impossible to love—one that revealed a small gap in between her two front teeth, presumably from neglecting to wear her retainer she had following braces. "It makes me have a lisp, Alec," she would always say. It's safe to say that Alec has always been in love with Rose, but Rose has never loved him—at least he didn't think so. She always had this charisma that attracted everyone to her, that along with her carefree personality. It made it almost too easy for everyone to talk to her—too easy for everyone to fall so deep in love with her.

Alec was nothing short of a saving grace in her eyes. He would always ask "how is my rose" whenever they would see each other or whenever he wanted to see how she was doing. He was so handsome, even if he didn't think so. His presence was so soothing, and any uneasiness that she was feeling just disappeared when he walked into the room. He was such a gentleman, the exact opposite of every guy she had ever been with. His dark brown hair curled by his neck and fell just above his eyebrows. She loved how he would glide his fingers through it to move it away from his eyes. His dark brown eyes witnessed her breakdowns and always had a look of concern and sympathy. His face always had a little stubble on it, even if he shaved that day. It had no flaws except for a small scar above his right eye. He claimed he didn't know how he got it. His smile—oh God his smile. She loved how it made his eyes look. They would always get squinty whenever he smiled, so much so you could barely see the dark brown color. His teeth were perfect, presumably from wearing his retainers after he got his braces off. It's safe to say that Rose has always been in love with Alec, but Alec has never loved her—at least she didn't think so. He had a charming personality and he always knew the right thing to say. It made it almost too easy for everyone to talk to him—too easy for everyone to fall so deep in love with him.

The blanket was soothing on her bare skin. The blanket and sheets that smelled like Tide were pulled over her bare body and clung to her, hugging her curves. She laid on her back and welcomed the morning sun as it began to light up the room. Her mind this morning was content. There was only one person she wanted to see, and it was the person she had sex with last night. She rolled to her right and saw him, saw the one person she wanted to see: Alec.

Blue Bird
Allison Astorino

The sun was just starting to peek over the bare branches of the trees that surrounded them. Cold, sharp air filled their lungs as each of them breathed heavily, looking forward at the scene before them, now starting to become illuminated by the light of day. Something was shifting. The horrors they had faced, the things they had seen, the abomination they had all felt a part of was beginning to drift away. They were all thinking, could it be that easy? It wasn't. The colder air bit into their skin, the colder the body looked in front of them. It was slowly freezing, the life having left it a long time ago now. How could it be a long time, it was just hours. Yet, it felt like years. And they knew that the in a few years, it would only feel like hours. It brought most of them to tears.

Kit sunk to his knees, unable to hold up his body anymore. He was so tired of being strong, being vigilant for so long. The snow allowed him to sink a little, and it came around him, hugging close to his body. In the midst of the sunrise, it glittered in all the places it laid undisturbed. It looked beautiful. Glorious.

Suddenly, the silence of their shared moment was ripped apart by a large group of fluttering and flapping wings. A few of them took wild steps back, surprised and bewildered by the sudden motion, their bodies still ready to fight, still responsive as ever to the slightest movement. Would that go away?

Birds, feathers so blue they were darker and more pure than the sky, decorated the space between the living and the dead. None of them had noticed the seeds before that moment, but now they all looked on, both entranced and horribly confused, as the swarm of birds settled gently on the packed snow, pecking at the seeds that someone had taken the time to spread out in intricate patterns. Eliza breathed the words of a question, but no sound actually escaped her lips. She wanted to know who, and why. Leslie shook his head next to her, feeling like he had heard her question, but not being able to verbalize an answer. The black liner around his eyes had spread down both of his cheeks, and he looked more harrowed than ever before, like some dark entity that had escaped a cruel cave. She couldn't even look at him, let alone lean into him like she had wanted to not minutes before, when the sun was still hidden below the horizon.

The birds continued to eat, pecking the ground, hopping around and creating soft footprints in the snow, barely disturbing it at all. The ground still sparkled, untainted by their presence. Tears rushed from Kit's eyes, but he wasn't sure why. Was he just cold? Was he sad, or angry? He didn't feel much, mostly just numb. Exhaustion, that was the only word that came to his mind. It wasn't enough though.

Milo sat down next to him, his own legs trembling before giving out beneath him. He let out a little gasp as he fell, the weight of what they had seen, what they knew, and what they had done crushing him to the ground. As effortlessly as the birds had landed before them, Kit wrapped his arm around Milo, pulling him into his heavy coat, into his chest, his hand against the back of Milo's head, pushing on his wet and sticky hair and holding him close to himself. They both wanted it; neither resisted.

Charlotte Cooper was the only one who could not be quiet. She looked at the birds before them, breathing heavily, not from exhaustion, but from rage, from a need to move, to run out at them. Something was running through her veins, pumping adrenaline throughout her entire body. In that moment, she felt she had no blood, but something else. She wanted desperately to be separated from whatever horror they had been a part of. She denounced it.

She screamed.

The birds didn't move. Some looked over at her, but most kept pecking the ground, eating the seeds. She ran out at them, moving her arms wildly. They flew up and out of her way, circling her, cawing loudly, their blue feathers flapping widely in the moment. The rest looked on, feeling stunning, but also feeling like they couldn't understand it. Charlotte looked back at them, at all of their dead eyes blinking back at her. She quieted down, standing in the middle of the seeded field. She turned around, looking at the body at the other end of the field. The birds stayed away from it, too. She sank down to her knees in the midst of all of them, and they settled down around her, pecking at the seeds, continuing to eat, to bathe in the warmth of the rising sun. The sun kept rising. It didn't stop.

All of them looked at her, in the midst of the field, in the midst of the birds that were all blue, with pointed heads and black tips. She looked just like them. In blue jeans, her platinum white hair peeking out of the black hood of her coat. She sat crouched down, sitting on her legs, her feet spraying out on either side of her body. She was hunched over, looking at the birds, touching the seeded snow before her. A bird wanted it, and she threw the seeds to it. It ate greedily.

Milo let out a loan moan, then a sharp cry. His body shuddered, he couldn't keep it in. Kit held him tighter to his chest, encircling his whole body with his two strong arms. He wanted a drink. Eliza tied her hair back, pushing her bangs out of her face, not wanting to look at her honey hair anymore, filled with spots of red. Leslie stood taller next to her, for her. She didn't need it, but she noticed, and she appreciated it. For a long time, together, they looked out at Charlotte in the field with the birds all around her. They watched her and her curiosity about them. They thought she was just like them, those colorful birds. Living through it all, and coming back for more, needing it somehow.

She looked out at them, eyeing her. They were different, needing something extraordinary to make it all worth it. She looked up at the rising sun that was warming her skin. She was different. She had lived. And she was thriving.

She took some seed out of her pocket, and tossed it out into the sunlight, watching it fall on the glittering snow, watching the birds eat.

Serendipity
Kelli Rajala

She walked into the café and shook the snow from her jacket, kicked it off her boots. Her cheeks and nose were flushed bright red and her hair was screwed up from the hat she had been wearing. She still looked beautiful, however, if not a bit sad. I watched her sit at a table in the far corner by herself. When the server came by and asked if she wanted coffee, she nodded.

I stopped at the Green Ground Café every weekday after work and so did she. Sometimes I would run into people I knew, or they would come to see me, knowing this was my habit. However, she was always alone. I felt weird watching her as often as I did, but for a long time I was too shy to even consider saying hello. I honestly don't know what changed my mind on that frigid winter day.

Once the server came back to hand me my peppermint hot chocolate, I grabbed the cup and my jacket and walked across to the other side of the café. Before she even noticed I was there, I took the seat across from her and set my cup down on the table. She looked up with a blank expression on her face, as if having no reaction to my presence. One long, awkward moment later, the server dropped off her coffee.

"Hi," I said quietly. She was now staring at her own cup. Her bangs covered her blue eyes. "Pretty cold outside lately, huh? Seems like winter's really been hangin' on this year."

She looked up, but there was no response to follow. I started to wonder if I was bothering her. Maybe this was stupid, me sitting with her. Who just sits with random people they don't know anyway? Maybe she thought I was weird. . . .

"Yeah."

My head snapped up. My eyes met hers, which were glued to my face, studying me.

"Huh?" I asked stupidly.

"Yes. It does seem that way."

In spite of the fact that she still looked sad, I found myself starting to smile. Once I realized this, I toned it down. Where to go next?

"Uh, yeah. It's . . . it's pretty and all, but I miss the warmth and sunshine of summer." She sighed, nodded. "Is everything alright?" I asked. "Would you like me to go?"

"No." There was a long pause where I wondered which question she was answering. "I mean no, you can stay."

"Okay."

On Thursday, she looked around the café for the first time when she came in. I waved and, still without a smile, she made her way over to my table and pulled out the chair across from me. Once she was seated, I waved down one of the servers for her.

"Think we'll see spring sometime this year?" I asked.

She shrugged.

"Sure."

She had ordered another coffee, but like the day before, barely touched it. It almost seemed as though she was simply accustomed to nodding when asked if she wanted one. I watched the steam dissipate over time as we sat in silence, the coffee losing its warmth.

"Um . . . so my name is Max, by the way." She gave me a curious look. "Yeah, I know. It's not even short for Maxine or anything like that. It's just Max."

She nodded as if she understood, though even I didn't understand why my parents thought Max was a good name for their daughter.

"Elle," she replied.

"Like the letter?"

Her mouth twitched. She had almost smiled.

"Yeah. Basically."

"Are you always here?" she asked on Friday as she sat down. I nodded. "I've never noticed you before."

"You always seem so down, in your own little world," I answered.

"You've apparently noticed me, though."

I felt my cheeks flush.

"I mean, I suppose so."

"Why did you sit with me?" she asked.

I thought about it for a moment.

"I . . . I don't really know."

Another mouth twitch.

"That's a pretty terrible answer."

I let out a short giggle.

"Yeah, sorry. You're right. I guess I just thought, you know, since we're both here every day it would be nice to get to know you. Maybe then, you wouldn't have to sit alone. I mean unless you like sitting alone. I suppose I shouldn't just assume . . ."

This time I got an actual smile and, although brief, it warmed my heart a little to finally see a happy look on her face. It could have melted all the snow outside for miles.

"It's okay," she assured me. "I do like the company. I'm glad you sat with me."

"Me too."

Toward the end of our small conversation, she pulled a scrap of paper out of her pocket and flagged the server down for a pen. She wrote her number down and handed me the slip of paper.

"It's the weekend tomorrow," she said. "So . . . if you want, well . . . you know."

I didn't have much time to think of a response, as she was already bundling back up and grabbing her things as I sat dumbly staring at the paper in my hand. I looked up just in time to catch her wave at me before she disappeared out the door.

It was rather forward of me, but on Saturday I asked her if we could hang out, particularly somewhere other than the Green Ground Café. To my surprise, she actually agreed, and so we ended up meeting at the local used bookstore, a favorite spot of mine. As it turned out, the small shop was also one of her favorite places in town. We perused the bookshelves, occasionally pulling out books we liked and recommending them to each other. I learned that she preferred to stick to the classics, where I typically went a little more contemporary.

"I've never really seen you around before, outside of the café I mean, and I come here a lot," I noted.

"I don't usually have much time outside of work," she answered.

"What do you do?"

"I'm a set designer."

"That sounds like fun."

She shrugged.

"It's okay, I guess."

"Not what you wanted to be doing?" I questioned.

"Not exactly." She sighed. "I used to be one of the set painters, but now I'm collaborating with the people who do the actual work on props and construction and all that . . . and the painters."

"Why don't you paint anymore?"

She looked down at the floor, the sadness returning to her face. She asked me to hold out my hands. I did as I was told and wrapped my own cold hands around hers.

They trembled.

"Idiopathic peripheral neuropathy." I gave her a shocked look, surely showing my heavy level of concern. I didn't know what to say, though, which she seemed to understand. "My mother was a painter, before she passed away. I guess you could say that I inherited that gift from her. On the side, when I wasn't painting sets, I was selling art in galleries."

"I'm sorry. I can see why you've been upset."

She shrugged.

"Hey, I appreciate you caring, though. It's meant a lot to me. Seriously."

She pulled a beat-up scrap of paper out of her pocket and tossed it into the nearby garbage can, and then walked away toward another bookshelf. I followed behind her, but not before catching a few words scrawled on the discarded note.

Dear Family and Friends,

I'm sorry I just couldn't do it anymore . . .

Fatherland
Wade Holcomb

This is the decision I have made. It is my own. William wrote in the letter in his hand, closed it, and returned it to his pocket. He remained stoic in his seat beside the office door while the surrounding people ceaselessly stirred. The clattering of typewriter keys and shuffling papers had put William in an almost trance-like state. He stared off into the window at the opposite end of the room. On the oak tree outside, he spotted a cardinal perched on one of the branches. It flitted from one branch to another in a way that made William smile. Watching the cardinals dance on the branches outside of his bedroom window was one of his fondest moments of growing up.

These little simplicities have been left with a taint of uneasiness for William in the wake of the Japanese attack on Pearl Harbor. The collective tension of the country had washed its way to William's farmhouse in Strasburg, Pennsylvania, where his parents had fallen victim to the mass hysteria. His parents had lost any semblance of joy that they once had once the war had broken out. Being born in Frankfurt, Germany, they had witnessed the horrors of war first hand. His father still bore a scar on his cheek from the shrapnel of an American grenade. The scar stood as adamant as the misguided beliefs with which he left the war.

"Of course the country has been attacked! Roosevelt and his Jew loving pigs have put us all at risk! *Verdommte Juden!*" His father shouted the morning William left. *Juden . . . Juden . . . Juden . . .* still struck his ears like a switch. Each step along the road where he was walking, William heard his father's voice . . . *Juden.* He never understood the hate behind his father, but he reconciled that it must be the remnants of a different time. He continued his walk to town, hands in his pockets, replaying his father's words over and over. . .

In the office, William's trance was broken by a familiar face that passed his gaze. The sand-toned hair, the square jaw, and the flicker of a smirk drew William to his feet. His brother, Fredrick, was there! He could not believe what he was seeing! Before he had fully risen, he sat back down again, as he had seen that the man was not his brother. William placed his head in his hands in embarrassment. His brother was fighting in the war in Europe. He had joined the German military at the outset of the conflict at the compulsion of his parents. They had told Fredrick that he should be "defending the Fatherland." He left to join them out of his duty to his parents. William had not seen Fredrick in almost two years. The cardinal reappeared in the window across from William, and slowly William was placed in the trance once more.

This duty to serve the Fatherland was not isolated to Fredrick. William had been pressured to fight for Germany as well. That decision was what pushed William to leave that morning. It was difficult to rationalize going to war for an ideology of hate and fear, despite the commendation and respect his father would bestow on him upon returning . . . if he were to return. He put his head back into his hands at the thought.

Only one person he knew was vocal of their displeasure of the war, and that was his love, Dorothy. She was openly critical of the Nazi regime and the invasion of Poland. She was furious to find out that William's brother had left for Germany.

"I cannot believe that he could just blindly follow along with all of this. Does he not see how hateful it is?" Dorothy inquired.

"He just didn't think about it that way," William tried to justify. He had gone to visit Dorothy the morning his father pushed him to enlist. She always had a way of calming his nerves. This was not one of those mornings. "They—they're actually asking me to enlist," William as able to mumble.

"You are going to enlist with the Nazis!" Dorothy exclaimed.

"I never said I was joining, but that they have asked me to enlist," William clarified, "But it wouldn't be an all bad thing. I'd get paid, I'd bring respect and honor to my family . . ."

"Respect and honor? No, there is no honor in fighting a war to continue pushing hatred. You are an American. Not a German. You would do nothing but shame yourself," Dorothy retorted as she turned from William. Dorothy's braided black hair wagged behind her as she shook her head in disbelief.

"Dorothy, please . . ."

"No! You should know better than this. For God's sake, you can't even make a decision on your own!" With those words, Dorothy departed. It was the last moment that they had spoken since.

Can't even make a decision on your own . . . her words boiled in his head. He looked at his fingers as if he would find the answer at the tips. There would be a loss with either decision, but which loss is greater to him: A loss of dignity or a loss of the only support he had ever known? His thoughts then swept back to Dorothy and how he admired her passion and independence. He closed his grip and prayed that he was making the right decision.

He withdrew the letter from his breast pocket, took the pencil therein, and scribbled the last few lines; *This is the decision I have made. It is my own. I am sorry, Dorothy.* He returned the letter to his pocket as the office door opened. A man stepped out dressed in his standard olive drab, the name Lt. Albertson imprinted on a tag on his chest and addressed the now standing William.

"Are you William Fuchs?"

"Yes, sir."

"Alright, let's talk about getting you enlisted in the United States Army, son."

A smile spread across William's face as he took a seat in front of Lt. Albertson's desk, and the recruitment office door was closed.

Corner Options
T. A. Majeski

Too many doors. My knee is bruising as it slams again and again on the underside of the table. Way too many heavy, locked doors and no more options. My pulse is a constant hum drilling into my head. I try not to look at the one-way mirror in front of me. The burning in my mind hasn't stopped. It should have, but now it's way worse, like it's had time to sink into my body. I can't shake the idea—it's shredding me—that everything is broken. The world is made of broken, sharp edges that cut into every part of me. It can't really be my fault that the antique dealer died, but that doesn't kill the nightmare.

I just barely resist the frantic need to slam my head into the table.

The door across the room opens and I jump, rising partway from my seat before the handcuffs jerk me to a stop in a half-crouch.

A man comes in and closes the door behind him. He hands me a paper cup half filled with coffee and sits down. The chair creaks.

The man consults a near-empty file. "Mateo Estrada?"

I consider lying, just to mess with him, but there's no point.

"Yeah."

The man extends a hand. "Peter Ritter. I'll be your legal counsel."

I don't shake.

The lawyer rolls his eyes and withdraws the hand. "Gangsta. Fine, bro. Why did you decide to rob—" he checks the file, "—Brian Zielinski's antique shop?"

I try to focus on the coffee cup, but the whiteness of its paper—the color—it's way too familiar. I switch to staring at the scuffs on the table to avoid looking at the one-way glass. I try not to think about the robbery. Doesn't work . . .

. . . I jimmy the shop window. I have to think about important things, wearing gloves, putting my mask on, only grabbing cash and jewelry, but my brain feels like a balloon straining with too much helium.

The window gives an angry shriek and I jump back, nearly dropping my crowbar. I suck in a deep breath. All I want is for this to be over, but my stomach hurts when I think of life on the other side of tonight. I wait for a minute to make sure an alarm won't go off. I kiss my scapular, trying to reassure myself. It's okay. He doesn't have an alarm. The shop stays quiet. I swing a leg over the sill and pull myself through the window before I have time to think any more.

Inside, the shop is surprisingly bright with moonlight. I feel exposed. I move to the cash register, weaving through old chairs, wardrobes, and bedsteads. I pry the register open quickly and jam the contents in my pockets without bothering to count. The wads of cash feel slender and wispy in my hand. I see my fingers are shaking. I don't need to be scared. For the hundredth time, I picture the owner of this shop giving that fifty to the panhandler who everyone in the neighborhood knows isn't actually blind or a veteran. Zielinski gave Sergeant Heely that money, even though he had to know Sarge was faking. He is a very kind, generous man. That type of man wouldn't mind too much if I take a little money and jewelry. I feel my hands steady just a little at the next thought. And even if he did catch me, a man like that might not even press charges.

As soon as I can trust my hands, I move to the jewelry counter. There is an expensive lock on the glass cabinet. I ignore it and break the top of the counter with the crowbar. The glass shatters with a muted groan and clatter. I reach in to grab a handful of the dimly shining silver and gold bracelets.

"What are you doing?" I swing around, spraying scraps of glass as my sleeve drags across the broken remains of the countertop. A man stands there, blond hair searing white in the moonlight. A light comes on and I can see the surprise in Mr. Zielinski's face.

"You're the guitar player from the street—Mateo?" I feel fear shoot painfully from the base of my skull to the pit of my stomach. How does Zielinski recognize—? I put a hand up to my face and find it moist and naked. I've forgotten the mask. I look at Brian Zielinski helplessly—I think part of me wants to be told what to do next. Finally, I remember I have a voice.

"Don't call the police!" My voice is pitched high enough to hurt as it comes out.

Zielinski looks surprised and I feel a soothing flare of relief. "Why would I—"

Zielinski's eyes go to the crowbar on top of the jewelry case, the glass that covers the floor, the bracelets I have dropped. His expression sharpens into anger. "You damn little shit. Are you robbing me!"

My heart goes into overtime, forcing confusion through my body. *No, no, no.* My view of Zielinski's anger is blocked by drifting clots of blackness. I lean on the broken counter, closing my eyes, trying to understand, trying to pull in air. Why's he this angry? It doesn't make sense. When I look up again, Zielinski is holding a phone. "Hurry up. I'll hold him until you get here."

My body flashes cold then hot. "You called the police?" I ask, though I already know.

I start to back away from Zielinski. The window is the only thing I can think about now, the only way to fix this nightmare. But Zielinski guesses what I'm thinking and moves between me and the path to the window. There is no way I'll get past him because Zielinski is crazy big. I realize I'm begging, hardly knowing what I'm saying, just needing to put something between myself and what I see coming.

"Please," I get out, "let me go. I swear I won't bother you again. At least don't press charges!"

Zielinski looks even angrier. "You tried to rob me. Why wouldn't I press charges, you freaking little bastard?" He keeps coming until I'm backed up against a shelf.

Zielinski is inches from my face. I can smell the bitter sourness of his breath. I start feeling around on the shelf at my back, behind, above. I just need a way out. Zielinski won't let up.

"You think you can destroy my property and just get away with it? No way."

I'm flooded in panic, a surging, hot flow that makes this horrible, burning buzzing in my head. My hand, searching the shelf above me, meets something large and very heavy. The police will be here soon. I can stay and be arrested or . . . I think for a moment, then decide not to think at all—it's too hard. The pounding of my chest, the hot buzzing in my mind, are too strong. I tell myself I can't help it. This is wrong—

My hand grabs the heavy thing—a lamp—and I swing it as hard as possible into Zielinski's head. The lamp cracks and so does Zielinski's head. He falls and I stare at the body, its skull dented and spongy-looking. Dark blood is covering the white-blond hair . . .

. . . The lawyer is saying something. "So the lamp was on the shelf over you?"

I nod, afraid that if I try to talk any more the frenzy inside me will break out again. The world around me feels changed, feels toxic, and just existing in it burns me.

"Theoretically," the lawyer says, "you could have, I dunno, fallen against the shelf in the struggle, made a grab at the lamp for balance, accidentally pulled it down on the guy's head." The man rubs his pudgy hands together, his focus no longer on me.

"Hmm. It might almost make manslaughter. Won't get you off of course, but might swing you a plea bargain."

I stare at him, but my eyes aren't focusing. I'm gouging the backs of my own hands with my nails. It doesn't feel like I'm doing it to myself.

The lawyer is still talking. "Or, you were scared, probably felt threatened, you were afraid he was going to hurt you. Yeah! A jury might buy that. No way you knew what you were doing."

I finally look up to face this smug jerk, but my eyes land just over the man's right shoulder and on the mirror. I notice my scapular is hanging outside my shirt. Suddenly I'm very aware of its presence around my neck. Its weight reminds me of things—I stop thinking and I tuck it back into my shirt. All at once, I need to see what I look like after everything that happened last night. Slowly, I let my eyes focus on the reflection of my face.

I look like shit.

The walls of the holding cell they put me in are blank. No graffiti, no stains even. Nothing to look at or think about. The burning pressure in my mind still won't stop—it's actually getting worse. I'm still fighting not to think. Every time the same thought cycles around it gets closer to breaking through.

I can't think about last night. It all seemed worth it at the time . . . No. Not going there. I cross the room. I sit down. I stand up. I rattle the door, rub my face—it's all a blur. I just need to keep moving. Panic shoves me across the room again. I run my hand along the wall—it's an old tile, sort of antique— Shit! I collapse on the bench. My knees are hammering the air. Why did I— This time I do slam my head into the wall, smashing it back several times. It helps. The dizziness, the pain, it makes it harder to think. I become aware of a wetness at the back of my head and pull my fingers through my hair.

They come away bright red and sticky.

And the thoughts are out.

I don't want it to be my fault, it can't be my fault. Sensations and images from last night are eating my mind and now I can't help figuring out how they fit with me. I replay everything that happened.

Zielinski-he was threatening me, right? It was self-defense. I want to believe this. I need to believe this. I was scared.

I feel the fear all over again. That hot, kicking, screaming panic, that fear he would get me arrested . . .

Shit. My heart is beating so hard it hurts. Was that why I swung that lamp?

I'm scrubbing the heels of my hands into my eyes and trying to think now. The panic, it hurt, made things blurry, but did I actually think Zielinski was going to hurt me?

He had me backed against the shelf, telling me I was going to jail . . . I couldn't go to jail, had to get away, the panic was burning, I was scared of what would happen if I swung that lamp, but the fear hurt so much I decided I didn't care—

I feel like my stomach's been beaten with a baseball bat, and for a second I could swear my heart stops. I decided I didn't care.

It is my fault.

For a second, I think the guilt will kill me. My mouth has gone dry. I feel so lightheaded that I'm sure I'll hit the ceiling any second. I'm having trouble breathing—I tug at the neck of my shirt, and my fingers snag on my scapular.

As my hand closes around it, I don't really feel better, but somehow, I don't think that it matters. Clutching my scapular, I feel more solid, like it's a leash holding back the worst of the panic. I sit there, doing my best to breathe, for a long time. The guilt isn't gone and the world still feels broken into jagged pieces that are slicing me, but I think I can see how the pieces might fit, how it might get smoother.

Hands shaking, I kiss my scapular and wonder if they have confession in prison.

I <3 Waffles
Esther Haven

When Chanelle Casey's phone rang, she was sitting on her couch, in her immaculate little apartment, making origami waterlilies with her friend, Warren. But when she answered it, she had gone into the kitchen and huddled near the sink. "Hi Kelly," she said, hoping her voice didn't shake too much. You would think she would stop getting excited every time the social worker called. After all, Kelly always said the exact same thing: your birth mother isn't ready to meet you yet, I'm sorry; check back in a few months.

Chanelle had started to look for her birth mother as soon as she'd turned eighteen. She'd talked to her adoptive parents, then to the adoption agency, then to Kelly, who had put her name on a tracing list, and then to Kelly again after Chanelle's birth mother was found. After that, she spoke to Kelly every few months. It had been a closed adoption. If Chanelle's birth mother said that she wouldn't meet with her, there was nothing Kelly could do. Nothing that Chanelle could do either.

So, Chanelle had made a life for herself, a life that she hoped her birth mother would approve of. She was twenty-four years old, employed as a secretary at a good advertising firm, pursuing an assistance-free, debt-free business degree via an online university, and she was the president of the local origami club.

Yet, even with the life she had worked out of nothing for herself, she still needed to know where she had come from, she still needed to know of what stuff she was made.

"Hi Chanelle," Kelly answered, sounding more cheerful than her usual, professional tone allowed. "Good news. Your birth mother is coming to Lansing this weekend, and she's agreed to meet with you."

The butterflies in Chanelle's stomach began to flutter around. "Really?"

"Wonderful, isn't it? I know it's a drive for you, but it's the only weekend she's going to be in town. I'll be there for a conference anyway, so I'll be glad to facilitate things around my schedule. Do your adoptive parents still live in Lansing? It might be a hard time for you all if you decide to visit them while you're back. I suggest you don't."

Chanelle pushed her tongue against the crooked tooth on the bottom row of her jaw and felt the phone in her hand grow sweaty. They've probably forgotten I'm still interested in finding my birth mother, she thought. Her adoptive parents hadn't mentioned it since the initial conversation, and they hadn't seemed to care much anyway. Their faces now stared at Chanelle, grinning that Casey grin that only she didn't have, from gray frames on the shelf above the sink. They still displayed the same cluelessness toward her as they always had. She was very good at hiding things from them. "I'm sure it will be fine. Besides, my sister Janna has been complaining that I rarely visit. I haven't been back to see my nephew in a while. He's probably talking a lot more now."

Kelly was unconvinced, "Meeting a birth parent for the first time can be an emotional experience. You don't know how you'll react—"

But Chanelle thought she did know. Her birth mother would have a good explanation for everything, surely. They'd connect. Genetics would be enough to overcome any differences. By the time Chanelle finished her talk with Kelly, she had a plan for the weekend. She could pack tomorrow, work a half day on Friday, tell her boss a family emergency had come up, and drive back to her adoptive parents' house. Kelly had told Chanelle that her birth mother would meet with her Saturday, most likely, or Sunday. It would be too hard to wait until Sunday.

"Who was it?" asked Warren, who had strolled purposefully over to the kitchen.

He was the one thing that Chanelle couldn't plan out. She never knew what to say to him. He didn't even know she was adopted, much less how she felt about him. She didn't even know how she felt about him. "Family thing. I have to go home this weekend."

"What kind of a family thing?" he asked, leaning up against the refrigerator and putting his hands in his pockets.

Chanelle liked it when he did that. She looked away. "My mom wants to meet with me, just to talk about some stuff."

"She's always bugging you about something."

"It's fine. Besides, I haven't seen Nate in a few months."

"That's right, choose your only nephew above origami club," Warren joked. "Who will preside over the meeting if you're not there?" He slid down the refrigerator to the floor and stretched his long legs out in front of him, his black dress pants bunching up as he did, revealing his mismatched argyle socks. "That's right," said Chanelle, "I need to get the designs together for the meeting . . . if I print them off, will you take them?"

Warren raised his eyebrows and then looked away from in pretend indignation. "Hmph. I certainly will not. You will remember you did not support my run for Vice President. You can just ask Marge to cover for you."

Chanelle grinned and crouched down at Warren's side. "Come on, please?"

"Begs the person who demoted me to the snack brigade," teased Warren as he pulled his tie looser from his neck.

"Will you do it?" Chanelle asked, nudging his shoulder with her fist.

Warren caught her wrist and held it before she could draw her hand back. Chanelle laughed, and before she realized it, he had pulled her face was very close to his. With his other hand, he reached out to touch her. Chanelle didn't know why she pulled away, but she did. Warren reluctantly let go of her wrist.

"It's alright," he said.

"What?" she asked, catching her breath.

"I'll cover for you."

Chanelle stood and edged away from him. Warren didn't move. "When will you be back?" he asked.

"Sunday. At the latest. Probably Saturday night." She answered, her thoughts turning again to the weekend. Maybe even Saturday afternoon. She doubted if she would last long at her parents' house.

"Let me know if you need anything. If you need to talk or—"

"I will."

Warren came to his feet and brushed off his pants. "I guess I should take off."

"I guess," Chanelle responded. Did she want him to leave? They trudged over to the door. Warren slid his feet into his shiny black shoes and reached for his suit coat. Then he opened the door and walked out. Chanelle shut it behind him and put up the chain.

During Chanelle's drive east, she stopped once for gas and dinner and then drove straight through. It usually took her about three hours to drive from Chicago to Lansing, but three traffic jams stretched it into five. The porch light was on for her when she got home. It showed the walkway, even more cracked then she remembered, with two faithful bushes on either side of the steps. A little green tricycle stood upright in the driveway. It belonged to Janna's son Nathan. They practically lived at the house. In fact, Nathan had been born while Janna was still living at home. His toys were all about. Chanelle didn't see Janna's car anywhere.

She knocked at the front door but didn't wait for an answer. In the mud-stained foyer was Nathan, toddling toward her. Apparently, the only one to hear the knock. He came very close and to her wrapped his arms around her knees. Nathan smelled like maple syrup. His black, frizzy hair was matted down with it. She patted his little head and off it came on Chanelle's hand. The toddler wasn't wearing any clothes, just waddling around in a red superhero diaper and sporting an absurd little smile. "Watch George?" he asked.

Curious George was his favorite show. She almost reached for her iPhone to pull up an episode. But his hands were too sticky. "I don't have time right now, buddy. Maybe later. Where's Grandma?"

She was in the kitchen, the kitchen in which Chanelle had always been able to find a sink full of dirty dishes, macaroni and cheese with lots of extra cheese, green Granny Smith apples, double chocolate chip ice cream, and crumbs across the countertops. Her mother turned from the skillet where she was flipping a thick cut piece of bacon with a fork and gave Chanelle a tight, oppressive hug. "I bumped into Nathan in the hall," said Chanelle after she greeted her mother. "Are he and Janna staying overnight?"

44

"Tyrell is gone for a few days for work, and Janna didn't want to be alone," responded her mother.

"I didn't know busboys were sent away for work," responded Chanelle. She hadn't meant the statement as sarcastically as it came out, but there was no taking it back.

"Oh, he got a new job. Didn't Janna tell you? He got his CDL, so he's trucking now."

Janna came into the kitchen before Chanelle could respond. She was dressed in gym pants and a tank top, and her blond hair was tied back in a tired ponytail. She supported Nathan on her hip. "Tyrell's doing real good," Janna said.

"He's doing well," corrected Chanelle. "I'm happy for you. Maybe things will work out after all."

"Do you want anything, 'Nelle?" interjected her mother, who was busy with the waffle-maker. "After I finish with Janna's, I can make something for you." The Caseys always ate late on Friday nights, because their father always worked late, closing the factory. And they always had waffles. Memories of helping pour the batter into the iron came back to Chanelle with the sound of sputtering bacon fat. The waffle maker was so old it leaked, and she was never able to pour in the batter without spilling some. Janna, if she noticed first, would always wipe it away before anyone else saw. Their mother hated wasting waffle batter.

"I'm not very hungry. I stopped for a salad on the way."

"What did you say you were back for?" Janna asked, setting down Nathan and smoothing out her tank top.

"A visit," answered Chanelle, striding over to the sink. She turned the faucet and washed the syrup off her hands. "It's been a while."

"Yeah, it has," Janna said. "Too long," she smiled at her sister.

Chanelle smiled back, "I heard that you got your GED. That's great."

"We're so proud," said their mother before Janna could respond. "She's worked so hard."

Apparently, getting a high school diploma, and being valedictorian of a class, wasn't as much of an accomplishment, thought Chanelle, since that was what she had done, without much praise. Her sister had been working at getting her GED ever since she had dropped out of high school after having Nathan two years ago. "Are you going to start college?" Chanelle asked. "Bradley University has a good nursing program. You could probably still be a nurse, if you want. That's what you always talked about. I can help you apply."

"Give her a rest first, Chanelle," interrupted her mother moving to put her hands on Janna's shoulders. "She needs time to get everything straightened out, and Nathan is still so young. And with Tyrell's new job . . . no, it's better if she stays close to home."

45

"We'll see," said Janna.

"Here you are, dear." Their mother set down a plate full of waffles, heaped with bacon, maple syrup and whipping cream in front of Janna.

Chanelle waited patiently for her own waffles, which she knew her mother would bring her regardless of whether she was hungry or not (she only got two, to her sister's three, and a pitiful amount of whipped cream) and just when she got them, she wondered if her birth mother liked waffles and if she ate them, four squares at a time, like Chanelle did. She wondered if she had her nose, the nose that was just a little bit too big. She wondered what her favorite color was. She knew it was a silly thing to wonder about, but Janna and her adoptive mother liked pink, and she thought that maybe her birth mother liked—

"What are you daydreaming about? Janna asked you for more syrup, Chanelle," said their mother.

"Sorry," said Chanelle, handing her sister the white ceramic jug of warmed maple syrup. It was the real stuff, straight from the tree. That was one of the only things her father insisted on. Everything else in the home was an off-brand of some sort, but he had to have real maple syrup. "Dad's late," commented Chanelle as she looked at the glowing, green numbers on the microwave.

"He's picking up extra hours tonight," bristled their mother. She got up from the table and walked with her plate to the sink. She thrust it in with the other dishes and Nathan jumped at the loud clanking noise that it made. Then, their mother started washing the dishes; instead of waiting until the next morning like she usually did. She attacked them with soap suds and an old sponge, her shoulders held back straight.

Chanelle noticed a pile of unopened envelopes on the counter to the right of the sink. Her adoptive family never seemed to get anywhere, and if they started to, unexpected bills would creep up and pull them back. Their parents never said anything about it, but growing up, Janna and Chanelle knew when times were hard because their father would work late and their mother would do the dishes obsessively, with her shoulders held back like a wall. Sometimes she would say to Chanelle, "Work harder, just work harder. You can be anything if you work hard enough. I want you to do better." But her mother never said such things to Janna, and when Chanelle was younger she used to feel responsible for improving their situation on her own. And the expectations for her had only been raised when Janna got pregnant.

"What are your plans for this weekend?" Janna asked Chanelle.

"I have a meeting tomorrow evening—for work—but besides that I'm not sure," Chanelle answered. She scooped up as much of the residue syrup on her plate as she could with a fork and then drizzled it into the last of her four waffle squares. "What were you thinking?"

"Nathan and I are going to the park tomorrow, you're welcome to come."

"I'd like that, I have to get in another run this weekend."

Their mother turned with hands dripping, "Oh yes, how is your marathon training coming, Chanelle?"

"Half marathon training, Mom. It's going well."

"I thought you were going to do a real marathon this year."

Chanelle pushed her fork back and forth across her plate. "It was too big of a commitment with work and my classes online. I'll do the marathon next year after I get my Bachelor's."

"You have to stick with your resolutions Chanelle, you know that that's the only way to do things."

"I know, Mom," Chanelle said. After the marathon, her adoptive mother would undoubtedly expect her to do a triathlon, and then an Ironman. She wondered, if her birth mother had been there to witness her first 5k, if she would have applauded the achievement and not expected a greater one to come after. Perhaps Chanelle would know after meeting her tomorrow.

It proved to be a longer wait than Chanelle had planned. She didn't sleep at all in her old bed. Somehow the creaking springs had become annoying, instead of familiar, and the quilt, the pastel quilt that her adoptive grandmother had sewn for her, had grown too heavy above her feet. She'd never loved this house, or this room, not really, but she had liked the feeling of it being hers. She knew all the chips and cracks in the blue-gray painted walls, the red nail polish stain in the stiff carpet, and all the hair-flecked dust bunnies underneath her bed.

The next morning, after she had gone to the park with Janna and Nathan and watched her nephew swing, and had run several times around the one-mile track, Kelly had called to say that her birth mother could not meet with them until later that day. So, Chanelle went back to her parents' house and took an apple from the bowl on the table. Her father had just gotten up, and it was the first time she had seen him since she'd been back. He put aside the financial pages he was reading and gave Chanelle a big hug and a bigger smile, before going back to reading about the risings and failings of the stock market. She didn't really know why her father read the financial pages, it wasn't as if he had a stake in them, but like real maple syrup, it was something that was a part of him. She wondered what he would say if she told him that her friend Warren read the same pages that he did, and that he used them later to make water lilies, and owls, and other origami feats, to display on his mahogany desk in his high-rise office.

But she never talked about Warren to her family, not even to Janna. It wasn't as if she was dating Warren. His Louis Vuitton shoes took him places she would never be good enough to go. But he was her friend, he was a good friend. Maybe, someday, when her parents weren't around, she'd tell her sister about him. Her mother thought that the origami club was foolish and impractical and that there were much better ways of spending her time.

Maybe Janna would think that it was romantic to meet someone at origami club, even if they were just friends. Maybe they wouldn't always be just friends. Warren never gave up on anything.

After lunch, Chanelle took a shower, or attempted to take a shower. Her nephew's toys were strewn about the floor and in the tub and her sister's blond hair hung in a wad above the drain. Chanelle reached for a piece of toilet paper, gathered up the hair, and prepared to throw it in the wastebasket under the sink. There it was, on top of a dirty diaper, positive and unashamed. A pregnancy test. Again? Chanelle thought. It was going to be hard enough for Janna to go to college with a two-year old child, and it would be impossible with another baby.

Just then, Nathan opened the door and started for his toy cell phone on the floor. "Not now, Nate," said Chanelle, looking up from the open cabinet. She shut the door to the cabinet and picked up her nephew. She marched down the hall to look for Janna, and found her in the living room, lying on the couch, watching TV.

"Nate came in the bathroom," Chanelle explained, setting down her nephew.

"Sorry," answered Janna, not getting up.

"Why don't you ever watch him?"

"I was watching him, he snuck away. What's your problem? Did he break something of yours?"

"I just want you to watch him. He's your responsibility. You can't watch TV all the time and expect your baby daddy to do everything for you. Tyrell might not always be around. That's why you need go to college. You still can." Chanelle said. Then she saw Janna's expression. Her sister knew that Chanelle knew her secret.

"He's my husband," said Janna, her fingers toying with the simple silver band on her ring finger.

Chanelle tried to bite her tongue. She rarely fought with her sister, even growing up. "You can have anything you want."

Janna wouldn't look at her Chanelle, but she pushed herself off of the couch and went over to Nathan who had just found the TV remote and had started pressing the buttons. He had just turned off the TV. "Maybe this is what I want, 'Nelle. What's wrong with being a mom?"

"Janna," Chanelle said as she watched her sister cuddle Nathan. "I didn't mean that. I love Nate. But don't stay here forever, not with mom. Figure out what you want away from her."

She looked toward the door and noticing their mother framed, steaming, in the doorway. Then back at Janna and added, loudly, so there was room for mistake. "Don't let Mom tell you what to do."

Then Chanelle strode for the doorway and tried to push past her mother.

"You don't understand the situat—" her mother hissed, and Chanelle felt drops of saliva on her cheek.

Chanelle wiped her face with her hand. "Leave her alone, Mom. Just leave her alone."

Her mother stepped back as the red began to seep into her face, and she sputtered back, "Chanelle Ann Cas—"

"Just Chanelle," she interrupted, looking up at her mother, who was a good three inches taller. "It's just Chanelle."

"Don't you walk out. Finish this, you never finish it," her mother ordered.

Chanelle stopped by the kitchen counter, her hand on her car keys. "It's done. I'm done." Surely Chanelle would never get in messes like this with her birth mother. You get along with your family, that's just how things worked, or how they were supposed to. Chanelle's adopted mother never knew when to stop a fight, and that was bad, because she was always starting them. But this fight was over—it was Chanelle's right to stop it.

It was still a good two hours until the appointment, but right now she felt like driving. She didn't think she'd ever stop driving. Her fingernails bit into the fraying seams of the steering wheel as she wound about the old, pot-hole scarred roads. Her sister was still a kid. Chanelle shouldn't have even mentioned her precious Tyrell or college. Janna could do what she wanted. But their mother seemed to think that she could control her youngest daughter. After Nate was born, their mother practically forced her to drop out of school because it was what was "best" for Janna. Chanelle wondered why it was only Janna that their mother kept all cocooned up; she had practically shoved Chanelle out after graduation. There was something ugly in the whole thing. Chanelle had never hated her sister, never in all the time they grew up together; but she almost did during that drive past all of the old sights in their part of Lansing, past all of the old buildings that never changed in the ways that mattered.

Eventually, when her time was up, her wandering, circling drive took her to the café where she was to meet Kelly and her birth mother. Today, Chanelle determined, as she pulled into the parking lot, things would be different. This afternoon, she would know who she was, and she would form a connection with the only person who really could understand her.

It wasn't until she reached the door that she realized she was still wearing her running clothes and that she hadn't showered. She wondered if she should drive back home and change, but there wasn't time. Maybe she should go back home anyway. Maybe this wasn't the right time to meet her birth mother. What if she wasn't everything that Chanelle hoped she'd be? What if they didn't have the instant bond that—

Chanelle saw Kelly wave from one of the booths along the far wall of the café. The dirty, checkered floors echoed her footsteps. It seemed such a long distance to Kelly's table. But at least it was only Kelly; her birth mother must have been running late. A gum chewing waitress, who sported a stained apron, asked for Chanelle's order almost before she had sat down across from Kelly. She thought about ordering waffles with bacon on the side and with whipping cream and strawberries heaped up on top, but the time for the breakfast menu was long over. She ordered a glass of water.

"How are you feeling?" Kelly asked after the waitress left.

"Good," Chanelle answered, wondering how the social worker's tone could be so precise and nonchalant, as if this was something that happened every day. "Excited."

"That's normal," Kelly continued, nodding her head so that the hair in her tight ponytail bobbed up and down. "I'll stay for a bit to introduce you and then I'll step out. It might be awkward. Don't try to go too deep with her. You'll find that she'll answer most of your questions before you ask them."

Chanelle waited with her hands folded in her lap, but every time the bell on the café door tinkled, she'd turn around, rudely, and gape at whoever had just come in. After a few minutes, Kelly began to check her phone for the time and missed messages. Finally, a half hour after Chanelle had arrived, it felt like a day at least, Kelly's phone rang.

"Hello? Yes. I understand," Kelly said. "She's here now—what? Yes, I'll tell her."

Chanelle knew, from a glance at Kelly that her birth mother wasn't coming. "Wait," Chanelle gasped out, afraid Kelly would hang up. "Can I talk to her?"

"She wants to talk to you," Kelly said. "No, I understand," she continued, shaking her head at Chanelle.

Somehow, Chanelle felt that this was her last chance. She would never meet her birth mother. "Will you ask her something?" Chanelle said, straining to hear the sound of her mother, her real mother's voice over Kelly's steady, pleasant, "I understand."

Kelly gave her half-smile and a quick motion with her hand, as if to say, "Ask it quick."

"What is her favorite color?" It was a silly question, and why it slipped out then, Chanelle never knew. But after she had asked it, she didn't consider it wasted.

Kelly furrowed her professional brow but repeated the question anyway. Chanelle could tell there was a silence on the other end of the line. But eventually, Chanelle supposed, her birth mother must have given some reply because Kelly said, "Thank you. Goodbye," and ended the call.

"What did she say?" Chanelle asked.

Kelly reached for her purse and put her cell phone back into one of the pockets, "There was some business that called your birth mother back to where she lives. She said to tell you she was sorry and that hopefully, you both can meet at some point," then she stood up from the table and extended her hand to Chanelle.

"What did she say her favorite color was?"

Kelly let her hand fall to her side, unoffended. "Green."

"Blue is my favorite color," Chanelle replied.

After Kelly left, she sat there, in the booth, for so long all of the ice in her glass melted back into water. She wondered what else she didn't have in common with her birth mother. There was no reason to bother Kelly anymore. She didn't need to meet her mother. She had left her once, and stood her up once—that was enough. Chanelle knew now all that she ever really needed to know. Maybe her mother did have her too-big nose, but it didn't matter.

She took out her phone, intending to text Warren. She found another message from him. He'd been texting her all weekend, mostly things like: "i didn't mean to make things weird between us . . . again." She hadn't responded to any of them. This text read: "headed off to origami club soon. how's home?"

"Don't know. Things aren't really making sense to me," she replied.

He responded within a minute, "want 2 talk?"

"Not now."

"breakfast? Monday?"

"Can we get waffles?" she asked.

"whatever you want," he sent.

"A lot of waffles?"

"you like waffles?"

"I <3 waffles."

Chanelle went straight home after the café. Her dad was gone and so was Nathan, probably out shopping together. But Chanelle found her sister, still on the couch. The TV was off. Janna was sitting, cross-legged, with an opened can of water chestnuts balanced on her knee. A pregnancy craving, no doubt. Her mother was in the kitchen, doing the dishes. "Mom," she said. Her mother turned off the water. "Can I have a fork?"

"You might offer to help with the dishes instead of making more."

Chanelle pulled a hairband off her wrist and tied her hair back. Then she walked over to the sink. "I'll rinse."

Her mother moved over, poured a generous amount of dish soap onto a sponge and scrubbed at the few remaining plates, cups. When she handed them to Chanelle, she made sure their fingers didn't touch. She kept her hands in the soapsuds. "When are you leaving?"

"Tonight, after I talk to Janna."

"It's a long drive to Chicago; you should leave before it gets too dark."

Once the dishes were done, Chanelle stepped back from the sink, and her mother pulled open a drawer handed her a fork. That's the way things were for the Caseys—the work had to be done before anyone got what they wanted.

51

Chanelle went out to the living room and sat next to Janna, and held out her fork toward the dwindling jar of water chestnuts. Janna smiled and put the can on the couch between them.

Thébaïde
Michael V. Gibson

At the east end of Bolshoy Prospekt stretched a block of shopfronts lost behind decades of smoke-stained cladding and neon signs, probably dating from the last revolution. I kept my head down as I passed, shielding my face against the worst of the cold. All day I'd been wending old streets and courtyards, not really looking for or expecting much. Eventually I came to the canal that bisected the city, and I followed its curvature through warrens of disposable apartments, broken alleys, empty parks. There were no people.

Up ahead, where the tenement blocks were stained the color of an old tooth, a series of jagged monuments lined the embankment. They honored minor revolutionaries, men and women whose names even the locals had forgotten, and each statue had fallen into rust and ruin. Phone numbers for gray-market services were stenciled across every surface. The nearest one depicted the continents on a cage-like globe, though its inscription had rubbed off and so had its meaning. Next to it, a Brutalist family posed against a banner, which said something about class struggle. Maybe someone had been proud of these things once.

For a while I puttered around the statues, trying to decipher this graveyard of ideals and promises. But I was an outsider: very little of this narrative made sense to me. Eventually I went back to the railing and watched the city disappear in the snow.

A pedestrian emerged from the haze. A woman: I caught a brief glimpse of her face behind her scarf and wool hood. She moved with hard determination, and I expected her to pass by and disappear into the fog like all else had. But she slowed when she approached the monuments, so I went back to the embankment to give her some privacy.

I waited a few minutes. When I turned around again she was still there, looking up at one of the statues. For an instant our gazes met, and maybe she wondered what I was doing here. I didn't have an answer to the imaginary question: I was just wandering, riding subways and buses and kicking around snowy alleyways and icy courtyards, looking for a moment that I'd lost somewhere in the intervening years.

It was too late to pretend we hadn't noticed each other. I nodded hello and pretended to inspect another statue—this one a child reading a book, but it was hard to tell for all its undisciplined cubism. The inscription was mostly covered by a smear of ice, and the few visible characters made no sense without context.

The woman crunched through the snow and came up beside me.

"Do you know what you're looking at?"

Her English surprised me. Only her rhotic vowels betrayed a trace of her mother tongue.

"No."

She pointed to a monolith with a trio of revolutionaries carved on its face, triumphant fists raised toward an angular sky.

"When my father was young, they came to his house." She sighed, and for a long time I wasn't sure if she were going to say anything else. "His parents buried their gun and burned all their books. That way they didn't have to go to the camps, when the soldiers came." She rapped the statue with her knuckles, and its hollow clang hung in the air like an open secret. "Everyone was starving."

She pulled her hood down, revealing a sad-eyed, wind-burned face. Her black hair snapped in the breeze, covering and uncovering a small crescent-moon scar on her forehead. She was probably my age.

"I don't really know what any of these mean," I said, my frozen lips barely able to enunciate.

"You're American."

I shrugged.

"My friends all wanted to go to America." She looked for a moment across the statues. "But I don't think it's better there."

I wanted to ask her why she was telling me this, but I already knew. She wasn't the first person who'd come up to me and treated me like a walking confessional. I was a foreigner, a disposable person, and as far as anyone knew I'd be gone tomorrow.

"Why are you here?" she asked.

"Just going for a walk," I said, deliberately misunderstanding the question.

"You have some kind of job."

I just shrugged.

"I ended up here."

She squinted, struggling to comprehend the expression.

"What is ending here?"

The wind died to a whisper and the coal smoke settled in. The city lay still in a slow fatigue of sickness and rust, and I tried imagining this neighborhood in the colonial days—empty fields, a tangle of train tracks, barrack housing for the countrymen who'd come north out of desolation and famine to build the Russian railroads.

"What are you doing here?"

"The bus." She pointed back toward Bolshoy, the last bus stop before the sprawl collapsed into pockmarked countryside and industrial scrubland. "It's broken. I think it's faster to walk than to wait for another one."

For the first time she looked me directly in the eye, and the city reflected in her eyes was a vision of devastation. She knocked on the soldier statue again, and there was something compulsive about it, as if she were verifying that the soldiers hadn't come to life.

"The bus is always broken. Everything is always broken."

"Take a taxi."

"I can't afford always to take taxis." She sighed and looked away. "It doesn't matter. There are no taxis in this weather."

Steam rose slow as yesterday, obscuring all, and across the faces of the year-blackened tenements loomed a permanent shadow of loss. Did her eyes reflect the city, or did the city reflect some atavistic sorrow in her eyes?

"Where are you going?" she asked, hesitating a little. "I never see foreigners here."

I pointed downtown, though in truth I didn't know where I was headed.

"I'm going that way, too."

With half a sigh she turned back to the city's melancholy dream. Frozen in the golden smoke was a kind of finality, and in the haze of snow and fog a mirage of buried memories and wasted years. The rush of high-rise development spiraling outward from the city center was a fantasy, just as unreal as the plastic cladding and cheap facades layered across all these crumbling buildings, hiding the brickwork but not disguising a single inch of decay. For a long time I stared like St. Anthony in the desert.

"You're going to work?" she asked.

For a long time I didn't say anything.

"Think I might get a coffee."

I leaned over the railing. Up and down the waterway a season of trash was preserved in the ice like fossils in amber.

"I've never had coffee," she said.

"There's a place. A few blocks that way."

She nodded.

We hesitated a moment and began walking along the canal, following an architecture of revolution, failed uprising, occupation, liberation, faded empire. The sun in the smog was an apocalypse of gold.

"The weather is bad today," she said, as she coughed on the coal smoke. "The weather is always bad."

We were heading nowhere and tracing an empire line—here the elegant Art Nouveau gave way to blocky communal apartments, there a fanciful Russian bungalow sat shoulder-to-shoulder with a sagging shantytown—and for a long time we said nothing, knowing neither each other nor where we were headed, except that our broken paths were entwining slowly, irreversibly, and tomorrow receded further and further into the smoke, and into ruin.

Snowstorm
Dan Jones

The first grade teacher appears pregnant. She is not. She appears fifty. She is ten years younger. She looks devilish. She is Catholic. Her glasses focus her beady eyes. Beady because they look like beads. Beady because they are piercing like the classroom dictionary says, but more because of the dictionary's description of a bead.

The third boy in line is looking at her pop-out stomach because he always does. Because he loves Dr. Seuss' "Hop on Pop." The boy at the back of the line is looking at the beads behind the glasses.

"Be!" she says. "Quiet!" she shouts.

The irony is lost on the entire group. A tired, grumpy dad in the lobby smiles behind his scarf.

"If you continue to talk . . ." she diaphragms.

The first grade teacher's class of kids are not brats. Her class of kids are excited about the early dismissal. Noon.

Don't be excited about the announcement is the intended lesson of the day.

There is going to be a snowstorm coming. It is on its way. Noon.

"Zip it, Kyle!" she says, zipping up her own thin lips. And Kyle thinks of the Grinch, because he's that third boy in line.

Two girls are clicking their shoes.

The first grade teacher looks at their shoes and their faces. Their faces stop the smiling and look at the teacher who hasn't smiled yet this morning. They do not look at their shoes.

It is only 9:28 a.m. The announcement was a surprise for everyone. The students did not know about a storm. The parents would be surprised–some disappointed about coming home, others excited to watch Christmas movies on the couch with cocoa and maybe some cocoa with red wine (for the parent). The teachers were also surprised.

The school cheered minutes before the first grade teacher exchanged the hallway joy for bathroom break instructions.

Kyle was excited to have a snow day and whispered, "Snow day," to the ugly girl with the cute personality.

"Kyle! What did I just say?!"

He wasn't listening. He did not care. The first grade teacher did not remember what she said. It had something to do with being silent in the hallways.

The class calms down because they are warned about losing their bathroom break if they do not calm down, and Kyle cannot calm down because he wants to urinate in the snow with his dad like he did on the last snow day. Kyle says, "Pee" to Josh. Josh laughs.

The first grade teacher does not hear. She is sighing.

The snowstorm is coming. There is no stopping it.

At 10 o'clock, the class is doing what the first grade teacher is telling them to do. At 10:15, the class is not doing what the first grade teacher is telling them to do. The class will not do what the first grade teacher is ordering them to do. The first grade teacher is warning them, and she wants to tell them that she will cancel the snow day.

"Enough!" says the first grade teacher. "I will not have this noise all day."

She will not permit the noise merely because they are having a half day.

The snowstorm will end their day together, and it will not come early.

The first grade teacher says, "You will not be leaving early if you continue."

Kyle says, "You can't cancel a snow day. It's already canceled."

"You're wrong, Kyle," says the first grade teacher. "You want to know why?"

Kyle does not want to know why and does not want to hear her say anything. He stays quiet. This never works.

"You're wrong because the snow day isn't what is canceled. *School* is canceled. You're also wrong because I can keep you in this classroom if you do not listen to the rules."

"You can't keep us all day."

"I can keep you after class. Especially you, Kyle."

Kyle is quiet. Kyle does not want to stay with the first grade teacher after class. Her threat, to keep students with her, always works.

At 10:48, the class listens. At 11:02, they have fun.

The snowstorm has not arrived. The kids are in school with their first grade teacher for the remainder of the hour.

The first grade teacher is angry. She did not like what the boy near the closets did. She will move his desk next to her desk once they leave, and that will stop him from doing anything to the closets tomorrow.

The first grade teacher tells others that she enjoys her job. She thinks she enjoys her job. She believes she enjoys her job. She wants to enjoy her job.

The first grade teacher had beady eyes when she was in first grade. Her stomach rose because of her unhealthy adult diet. Students have poked her tummy.

The first grade teacher sometimes cries at night.

The storm is going to keep the children inside of their separate homes. Kyle will not be playing outside. His mother will not allow him. She will protect Kyle.

Recess was canceled. The first grade teacher also canceled reading time. Indoor recess was next to be canceled, and she cancels it.

Kyle does not care. The first grade teacher does.

She wanted to go outside before the snowstorm, but the school was not allowing it. She wanted to read to the children. She wanted to have indoor recess. She wanted the janitor to fix the closet door last week. She wanted the boy who did things to the closet door to sit near her desk because he was a good helper.

The first grade teacher does not keep them late. She said she would not, and she does not lie.

The first day of class, the first grade teacher told the students that she would never lie to them. She never has. She tells the truth and keeps her promises.

The first grade teacher cannot not lie her head on her desk and cry before the snowstorm. The kids in her class would see and hear her crying. She stands and arranges the baskets that had spilled at 11:20.

The students are wearing their coats and looking at the clock. The snowstorm is arriving at 1:00 p.m. School will be let out an hour before this. The students learned they were being let out before the snowstorm comes. The students learned they were in a safe environment because of this hour gap.

The students and the first grade teacher will be in their homes when the storm arrives.

The first grade teacher will be waiting for the storm by herself.

The bell rings for dismissal, a few minutes before noon. These minutes also speak of safety and teach preparation to the students.

In the hall, before the exit, where her students had run to their caregivers, the first grade teacher stands still. The students are gone by noon. They had exited the building, and the adults had waved *goodbye* and *thank you* and *I have her* and *be careful* through the glass.

Kyle's mother is in her car looking at her phone, waiting. Kyle has not left the classroom. He is behind. He is late. He comes rushing out of the room and bumps into the back of the first grade teacher. He hugs her goodbye.

"It's okay," he says. "I'll be here tomorrow."

A First Date

An Excerpt
Nathan Calkin

Mia pushed the plate away as Robbie swiped through his phone. "I'd love to go someday. I've heard it's beautiful."

"You should. The photos I took didn't turn out that good, but the sunset over the ocean was breathtaking."

"Breathtaking," she repeated to herself.

This is probably the best one I'll find," Robbie said, flipping the phone around in her direction. Mia was instead looking at a table at the other end of the restaurant. A family was being seated, two parents and their kids.

"Look at that," she said.

"What?"

"If you had kids would you take them to a place like this?"

Robbie thought about it. "I guess so. I mean, if you have kids you have to take them somewhere."

"I know, but not here. It's not like this place is super uppity but there are other places. More family oriented. Or get a sitter or something. I dunno. Oh, that is gorgeous," she said, now finally looking at his phone. She took it from his hand and swiped through the pictures, taking a pause for the good ones. "How long were you over there?"

"A couple of weeks in total, but there we were just a couple of days." Mia continued to swipe until she looked up and saw a visibly uncomfortable Robbie resisting snatching the phone back from her. She handed it back. "It sounds like a good time. I don't travel too often."

"Well, neither do I." Robbie checked what photo she stopped at before putting it away. "Do you like kids?"

"Kids are fine," she answered, looking back at the family. "Just not here, necessarily." She went to sip her wine but the glass was empty. "Do you think you'd ever want a family?"

"I think so," he said, "eventually."

Mia didn't respond right away. Robbie ate the last ravioli off his plate. "I'm not sure I would," she finally said.

"That's alright."

"I mean, it's not an automatic thing for me like it is a lot of people." Mia traced her finger around the glass. "They say it's great, but then I think about all the other stuff you could be doing instead. Like traveling and taking pictures of sunsets. I'm just not sure at what point you decide that you're done with your own life and now you're ready to make it all about someone else."

"I guess so. You figure out, though."

"Only 'cause you have to. I just don't think I want to have to figure it out. Not yet, anyway."

"Well," he said, "you've got time to think about it. You don't have to decide tonight."

"How was everything?" The server asked.

"Excellent," Mia answered. Robbie nodded his agreement.

"Would either of you be interested in dessert?"

"I don't think so, not tonight," Mia answered for them both. "Could you bring us separate checks?"

The server returned quickly with bills, the two paid with cash and left together. Outside the restaurant, Robbie checked his phone. "Do you live close by, or . . ."

"No, I'm just gonna call a ride."

"Are you sure?" Robbie asked. "I could call you a Lyft or something."

"It's okay, I've already got it." She grabbed the phone out of her bag and opened the app.

"No, come on. Let me take care of it. Look," he said and stretched out his arm. A yellow cab pulled up next to them. "The old-fashioned way."

Mia smiled. "Well, thank you." Robbie handed the driver a couple of bills through the passenger side window. "You're sweet," she said.

"No problem," he said, pulling in a little closer. Mia stretched up and gave him a peck on the lips. Robbie took a step back, sticking his hands in his pockets. Mia swung her back into the back seat and slid in. Robbie leaned through the doorway. "You know, I only live a couple of blocks down the road if you wanted to—"

"We're not sleeping together tonight."

"Oh, I didn't—"

"But I had a good time. We'll do this again soon." Robbie smiled and shut the door behind her.

The cab drove off, Robbie waving through the rear window until they turned the corner. Mia enjoyed a quiet cab ride home. She scrolled through her Instagram feed, liking the occasional photo of a cute dog or some scenic view. When they got close to her destination, she slipped off the heels and swapped them for the flats she had in her bag. She carefully stowed them away as they pulled into the driveway of a one-story suburban house outside the city.

Mia let herself in through the front door. "Mommy!" She was greeted enthusiastically.

"Hey, buddy," she said, tussling his hair and giving him a kiss on the head.

"Hey, babe," Ben said, two-year-old in hand. Mia gave him a peck on the lips. "How was book club?"

"Fine. Shelley had a little too much wine so I just took a cab."

"I would have picked you up."

"No, it's not a big deal." Mia slipped her shoes off. "Oh, you wanted me to pick up toilet paper. Sorry, I got totally thrown. I can still—"

"Don't worry about it. I'll grab it tomorrow on my way home. We've still got a couple of episodes left in the season I wanna get through."

"Oh God, I don't know if I can make it all the way tonight."

"Well," Ben said, "we'll see how far we get. But someone still needs to brush their teeth," he said, reaching down and tickling the young boy in his pajamas. "Lemme put these guys down and I'll come join you. Did you eat anything there?"

"Yeah, Jenny brought this really good flatbread. I meant to bring you home some."

"I'll take your word for it. There's still some pizza in the fridge if you want some."

"Thanks." Mia retired to the bedroom, tossing her bag into the corner. She slumped down on the bed, phone in hand. She shut her eyes and listened to the water running from down the hall. Her hand buzzed. She looked at her screen and saw a new message come in before setting it back down on the bed. She rested her arm over her eyes and took a big breath in.

The House to Himself
Luke Fortier

This little lizard was always trying to escape—jumping up all the sides of the terrarium, hoping one of those impassioned leaps to heaven might be the lucky one. Elliot had found it in the backyard one morning with another one, slightly larger, that now sat calmly in the corner of their new sanctuary, gazing for hours at a time at the wall with enviable intensity. Elliot had supposed they were mother and son.

He sat on the couch next to them watching with his cheek slumped into his hand, wondering how long it took lizards to die. Forcing himself up off the couch—he swore to himself he would get some work done today—he walked sluggishly to his room, the tail of his robe dragging behind, and sat down at his desk. His walls were filled with countless paychecks' worth of books and encyclopedia sets and other must-know materials. It was, he thought, the main reason he was still living with his parents. But they were away for a few days, and Elliot had been looking forward to the precious silence one must have in order to work.

What was it going to be today? Poetry seemed the best option: W.B. Yeats, he thought—yes, he was a real poet, and after all, one must have the proper influences. This, Elliot thought in this silent and repeating soliloquy, is why he had quit college.

He cleared the clutter off his desk and swiveled the chair around, just to the right distance. The front of the book was so mysterious: a winding staircase ascending from a drawing of a man riding on a dolphin, and then a dragon lurking menacingly throughout the bottom of the green cover. What did it mean? He was surely going to find out soon, but not without some tea. He got up again to go warm up the water, when he thought, "maybe I should write instead . . . Or maybe I should read Blake today—yes I should read Blake."

Elliot then heard a commotion in the terrarium. The little guy was still trying to make a break for it. "Amazing," he thought, "all day he's been doing this." He was beginning to think up a name for it when he heard a car pulling into the driveway. He went to the window and saw his older brother, Jeremy, walking up to the porch, as he groaned over his arrival.

The door flung open as Elliot had expected, with the additional "Lucy, I'm home!" that Jeremy always found so funny. "Where is everyone?" he asked.

"They went to the cottage for a few days," replied Elliot, waiting impatiently for the hot water to boil.

"Hmm . . ." Jeremy clumped his paint-stained boots to the fridge and began picking through the spoils of their absence. "What're you up to today?"

Elliot groaned silently now. "I have some work to do," he said, pouring tea and avoiding eye contact.

"What work?"

Elliot did not want to waste the energy yelling at his brother in defense of his typical day, so he changed the subject. "What are you doing?"

"Well," said Jeremy, leaning on the washing machine, "Karen and I got a babysitter tonight, and we were going out for some drinks tonight; wondered if you wanted to join." Elliot was silently devising ways to decline the offer. He loathed the idea of hanging out with Jeremy. Every time he did, Jeremy and his friends would get too drunk and make fools of themselves as Elliot would be stuck there, embarrassed and annoyed. But Jeremy was always offering a night out, and Elliot was always caught looking for the best way to say no. This time it was taking a while.

"But if you're busy," said Jeremy, "maybe another time." He waved goodbye and clumped his boots out the door. Elliot waited for the sound of the engine get out of hearing distance and then walked with his tea back to his room.

He put Yeats away and took out the *Complete Works of William Blake*, opening up the old thing and putting it to his nose—he loved the smell of old books. The bookmark rested on *The Human Abstract*. Halfway through the short poem, Elliot slipped into a daydream: what if he became a lawyer—there's some real tangible impact with a foot in the abstract and the practical, but what if he were a lawyer in Ireland? Yes, he could do that, that would be easy. Then in front of his wondering eyes appeared the blur of a rapid, Napoleonic lizard jetting to and froe. Elliot escaped his coma and jumped at it, scooping it up in his hands. He walked back to the terrarium where he saw a pair of pink tennis shoes at one end of the couch, and a mess of brown hair at the other.

"When did you get here?" he asked.

"Where's Mom and Dad?" she replied, her voice trembling a little.

"They're at the cottage for a few days."

"They have a cottage?"

Elliot rolled his eyes and dropped the lizard back into the box, the mother still sitting in the corner contemplating the wall. Elliot hadn't eaten for a while, and it was a good time to eat—after this he would shut the door and put white noise on or something, and get some work done today. He was scanning the fridge when Joanna threw her phone on the ground and her face into her hands. Elliot heard her sobbing and was tempted to walk slowly back to his room without her noticing.

"I'm sorry," she said through her fingers. Elliot approached her like a stray cat taking food from someone's hand.

"You alright?" he asked, in a way meant to incite a brief answer.

"It's this thing with Eric, I just don't feel happy with him anymore," she wiped the corners of her eyes, "I don't know what to do. I was going to talk to mom about it, but I just don't know what to do."

"Well, maybe you should leave him," he said, trying to be helpful. Joanna looked up at him, hardly believing what he just said. She disengaged, stood up and walked out the door saying nothing.

Elliot noticed the lizard was not jumping anymore. "Finally!" he shouted, throwing his arms up victoriously, "you've accepted it! Life will be a little easier now, little guy."

He saw Joanna's car pull away through the window, and paced with his hand on his chin, talking to himself: "I don't know how people expect to be happy living like fools." He remembered he was hungry and went back to the fridge but found nothing. "I should really be reading," he thought, "anything but Blake, though." The book went back on the shelf and Elliot looked nervously for another book that might be readable. "I should go out."

He got dressed in his finest sweater-vest and put on his autumn coat. Where was he going to go? Around the block maybe, but no, that was not very useful of his time. If he was going to enjoy his time alone, it was going to be productive. The museum then, if they're open, but it was so far away. He sat down on the couch trying to fathom a remedy to his ennui and stared at the little lizard through the glass. He felt something envelope him; his eyes sunk into his head, his body fell numb with it, and the house became still and full of shadows. "It's got me," he thought. His ribs began to shiver, and he held himself as he tried to keep from crying.

The door opened again, and Elliot sprang up, but it must have been left open—no one was there. Elliot closed it again and walked back to his room, determined to get some reading done today.

Providence
Chris Lawitzke

We went into the woods at the end of the day to sit before a cross-to Firebowl! My cabin mates and I would venture down a serpentine dirt road to a parting in the woods beneath a veil of trees. The sun slipping beneath the earth, casting shadows, creating exaggerated pillars of our youthful frames. We'd kick stones in our wake, like titans walking the earth from time immemorial, sending them racing forth with clouds of dust made amber in the light of the setting sun. A half-mile trek into the clearing: a place of whispers. We'd walk in groups of ten laughing and yelping accompanied by satellites drifting about us at variable distances. The politics of a cabin might find them there like lonely mountains crumbling into piles of dust as if they were the very stones we had kicked in our wake. Phil walked at a distance. We'd taken to hiding toilet paper in his sleeping bag and pillow. Taulson and I—walking to the bathhouse, on mission from the rest of the cabin—would steal great wads of the brittle paper to hide amongst his things. We'd race down the trails, over roots, hiding behind trees making a spying game out of our prank. His departure found our hands wriggling amongst his belongings stuffing white paper here and there.

Phil, though not fat, seemed to meditate the imaginary line between casually big-boned and obese. He was sometimes the butt of our pranks but was just as often in collusion with us and exhibited a mind primed for scheming. Glowing innocence, though, often found him singled out by counselors to tell the truth as to what had occurred and, inevitably, he would crack like too brittle ice. This was most often why we would punish him with toilet paper-For being the hero.

Being an avid reader of comic books, Phil's bunk was often strewn with various piles of glossy booklets. The fluorescent light that hung from the ceiling would throw wild photons onto the pages setting up momentary beams of light like cruel tendrils of dragon's fire. On too many occasions I would pass his bunk only to be temporarily blinded by Phil's maternal gifts from home. Often these parcels accompanied letters written in his mother's curvy script and balls of caramel corn reminiscent of Eve's doomed fruit. In one parcel, accompanied by comic books and corn, his mother had included a t-shirt with a Superman insignia in the center except that replacing the S was the figure of an ichthus with the word "super" placed in its belly. Phil, excited, pulled on the shirt standing triumphantly on his bed with his chest puffed out. To complete Phil's ensemble, Taulson had tied a red towel around Phil's neck as a makeshift cape. We all laughed as Phil's pudgy frame teetered unsteadily on the elderly springs of his bunk the fan in the corner blowing through the cape sending the red cloth rippling.

Though I hadn't read many comics, I always listened intently when Phil described his favorite issues. His descriptions, like Delphic visions, described a world of glory waiting to be had. Sometimes I'd lay in bed imagining myself mixed within the plots committing acts of the greatest skill. My name, synonymous with legend, forever chanted by so many would look upon me like a vision of Providence. The unfathomable power that I held in these quiet moments tempted the inner-most parts of me. Was it blasphemy to bask in such fiction? At what point did a hero transcend his power and become something more? Where did power end and godhood begin? Always these questions stirred within me. I wished to be free of temptation but it seemed always more present like a hardened cancer. Soon the dreams, no visions, coalesced into greater magnitude as I soon began to reevaluate my understanding of the scripture. Would it not have been better for God to end Job's life at the beginning of the bargain? Surely, I would never make a man suffer to prove a point . . . to satisfy my own pride! I appreciated Phil's stories but, quietly, I yearned for so much more. I needed more.

We walked through the woods, passing buttressing walls of autumn olive ensconcing vast legions of chalky birch trees into a clearing with benches in long rows that sat before a large roughly hewn cross. The cross stood, perhaps, twenty feet in the air and ten feet across. I'd always thought that it looked as though it had been burned as the wood had an ashen pallor. The birch trees, bereft of the shrub, made a white wall around the clearing as the fire moved wildly with desperate hunger.

In the darkness, counselors would weep as they told stories of their return to Christ standing at the cusp of the fire describing occasions of spiritual multitude and defeat. Mr. Natasha, a retired second division football coach, explained that he'd seen Jesus at a mixer for athletics faculty. He'd seen him sitting at a table looking calmly at the crowds.

He had a glow to him . . . I knew as soon as I set my eyes upon him that I'd seen Him! I knew I'd found my purpose!

Mr. Natasha wept as he recounted his salvation at the hands of Mixer Jesus. He encouraged our multitude to look in unexpected places for the face of God between the trees, among the piles of stacked wood.

When you see Him you'll know it.

I'd never imagined a corporal Jesus. All my conceptions of Christ were imagined from children's bibles I'd been given as a child. His Caucasian face seemed so welcoming and familiar. His image never seemed so real as the possibility was becoming in my mind. I began to tease away the abstract principality so that I might see his true face.

Of Taulson, Phil, and I, I gauged my faith as the strongest. Phil's still rested in a kind of metaphysical Santa Clause world. He seldom spoke about it unless called upon during bible study and then would simply paraphrase the passage and give a youthful polemic gleaned from an array of phrases echoed by his parents or the far-right media that peppered his home. Taulson could care less. Where Phil held a kind of sacred model inscribed by his upbringing, Taulson joyfully whispered small blasphemies. His discussion in bible study was rare and if called upon he usually played devil's advocate by disagreeing with the overall message that our counselors had prescribed. When discussing Job, Taulson stated that Job got a foul deal. One of the counselors, hearing this, instructed him about the greater message of Job's trial to which Taulson replied that even if Job was ultimately rewarded he was still wrought with a dead family and a hell of a lot of baggage. I understood Taulson's point, he'd lost his mom the previous summer in a house fire that had left he and his dad homeless. His dad, lost in grief, had taken to walking the streets leaving Taulson alone for days at the mercy of shelter hands. The reconciliation of forgiveness for strife seemed, in Job's case, like a far-reaching expectation.

As Taulson was about two years older than us and about to go into high school, Phil looked upon him as a kind of big brother as he was an only child of senior parents. Taulson sometimes indulged these feelings of Phil most often during times before bed when it was clear that the memories of his mother and the betrayal of his father floated closest to the surface of his memory. Phil might lend him a comic book or a clean towel when Taulson was without. He would reciprocate by offering knowledge about girls or other subjects much too taboo for Christian living. Other times, Taulson would eschew Phil's kindness for what he called The Trying of Patience. He accompanied this title with his own sound effects reminiscent of royal horns and crowds gone wild with awe. His game involved bating our cabin mates into arguments by being annoyingly contrary or by committing obvious thefts.

—You took my CD!

—No, I didn't.

—It's right there! You're holding it behind you!

—Oh, this? I'm inspecting it for cracks . . . the light isn't quite right . . . can't really see if there's any.

—Well, give it back!

—What?

—My CD!

—This is yours?! I'm sorry . . . I found this over by my bunk.

—No. You didn't!

—Sure, it was . . . What are you getting at? Are you calling me a liar?

—Yes! You just took it off of my bed! I saw you!

—What would Jesus do, man?

—He wouldn't have stolen something off of my bed then said He found it by His!

—You profess to know the will of the Almighty? . . . *tut tut tut.* Shame,

67

shame, shame . . . blasphemy is a sin, man.

On the walk back to our cabin Taulson claimed to see Jesus on the back of Phil's t-shirt. He demanded that we hang the shirt in the cabin as acknowledgment of the presence of Christ. Phil agreed and we hung the sweat-stained shirt high on the back wall. Our Counselor, Mr. Heilborn, had been called away during the day due to some type of emergency so we were left unattended for most of the night. Mr. Natasha had been assigned to make sure we were asleep at a certain time but most of the night we made a ruckus singing praises to Sweat Jesus. Taulson took to directing a kind of praise band except that we interjected awkward statements into the lyrics. We laughed and fake-wept in the presence of our idol. Our debauchery rang out into the night. As we continued our mock praise the cabin filled with the light strumming of a guitar. So melodious and inviting. Phil called our attention to it but Taulson dismissed him as an idiot and continued his exaggerated groveling. The music tapered away as I felt eyes on my back. Looking up, I saw an unmistakable face, all white, with high cheekbones and deepset eyes with a long dark beard. Like Mr. Natasha had said, I knew that this was the face of the Almighty. I grabbed Taulson to show him the figure. He looked from the shirt to me then threw his hands up into the air.

—You can see him, too?! Oh, Lordy! Camp food must be getting to you—brain scurvy, man.

—It's there, I saw it. Jesus was looking at me! It's not a joke, Taul . . . like Natasha said . . . He's there! Don't you see Him?!

—Sweat Jesus! Please, please save our friends from madness. Please stay your hand and let our friend's mortal coil be pure and without tainting!

I looked at the shirt again, the face gone, it hung loosely on the wall, yet I could still feel those eyes on me. That night I had dark dreams of eyes hanging before me, the pupils dilating into great dark pools. I looked and saw a great fire surrounding my cabin mates. They were screaming and carrying on with faces covered in varied shades of white and black. Taulson's face was smeared with pitch and charred wood. The dark gum, heavily applied to the hollows of his eyes, made phantom orbs that seemed to glow. He looked where I stood and, for a moment, I saw someone else behind his makeup. Taulson's ne'er-do-well countenance was overshadowed by something that looked upon me with palpable malevolence. The shirt, tied to a long birch branch, was waved to and fro over the flames. It seemed to me like the banner of a savage empire. The empire of the White Face. As I looked, Taulson handing over the banner to another member of the rabble, took a tattered book from a place I could not see then lifted it above his head. He shook the book causing innumerable pages scrawled in red script to fall into the maelstrom of fire. With the burning, a great sound began to exude from the ground as loud as a fanfare of Gabriel's horn. I held my ears and whispered a silent prayer that I might receive mercy. The company around the fire seemed deaf to the growing sound as the ground before me shattered. The clods of dirt, heading skyward, vaporized into the tiniest specks of light setting themselves into the sky like stars. I felt in myself the pull of annihilation as the sound turned from the audible into an all-encompassing breath of the White Face.

As I awoke from the nightmare I could still see the halo of the fire fading into the blush of my unopened eyes. Mr. Natasha knocked quietly then opened the door with the greatest care setting his eyes on the shirt clumsily tacked onto the wall. He stood looking up not saying a word his dark beard tapering to the middle of his chest like a large droplet of ink. He continued looking at the shirt almost as if he were enveloped in a silent conversation. His watch began to beep, and with a slight pause he began to sing.

—Time to get up boys! Time to get up . . . Time to get up . . . Time to get up in the morning! Up, up, up, up!

Taulson was the first to sit up in his bunk. He glared at Natasha then grabbed his towel and walked towards the door to wait for the rest of our cadre. We gradually joined him then ventured towards the bathhouse. I couldn't help avoiding Taulson's gaze. While we walked, he looked in my direction and smirked as though he were trying to communicate some iota of mischief. I couldn't help but look away as his gaze had so terrified me the previous night. A new fear stirred in my stomach. It stirred with Taulson's slight glance causing an unfamiliar ache. I had never feared him for we'd always been on equal ground but now his gaze was like the tip of a red-hot pin slowly working its way through my flesh.

I wiped away the fog that clung to the mirrors from the steam of the showers. My visage blinked at me from the mirror with great red eyes. I hadn't felt discomfort, nor did they itch, yet they were a deep red marked with a matrix of broken blood vessels that seemed to cast a pink glow about my gaze. Natasha walked behind me as I stared with mild panic at my reflection.

—Wow! Looks like you've got the pink eye.

—What's that?

—It's when you get something in your eye that's not supposed to be there or some kind of irritation . . . I'm better at offense than doctoring . . . Why don't you go and see Nurse Rosa on the way to breakfast. She'll want to take a look

Nurse Rosa, the camp nurse, was known for being quite secular even though our camp, Camp Wannapayke, was the foremost church camp in the Midwest. Her critiques of what she called "scenes in the woods" invited disdain by the other counseling staff. We could often hear them on quiet nights after lights out making jokes about her bent over figure or her strange way of injecting her inner-dialogue into the middle of her vast rhetorical conversations.

I approached the small building, the size of a carriage house, decorated with a large tin-red cross to the right of the door. The decor was a blend of decades ranging from the 50s to the late 80s. Two scratchy hot pink chairs sat in the waiting room with a multi-tiered coffee table strewn with old copies of *LIFE*, *Zoobooks*, *National Geographic*, and *Camp America*. The walls were hewn from rough cut planks with nails sticking out where they'd been haphazardly applied. A particle board bookcase stood on the wall behind the door that leaned dramatically to the left with giant first-aid manuals adorning the shelves with pages jutting in all directions. With the sheer mass of the shelves, it looked less like a bookcase and more like a first-aid golem awaiting summons. At the end of the waiting room against the wall stood a pedestal with a heavily marked first-aid manual above it a painted red cross. Nurse Rosa was talking on the phone in her office with the door slightly open.

—These things happen Mr. Sikes. We'll keep an eye on him . . . don't worry I've seen these things before . . . we just have to push fluids and we'll make sure that happens . . . you have to go? Of course . . . yes . . . yes, I can call you later this evening . . . oh no! It's not like there's anything going on over here . . . of course I'll give you a call. Goodbye!

—Why are you here?

—My eyes are bloodshot. Natasha told me to come and see you.

—MISTER Natasha.

—MISTER NATASHA told me to come and see you.

—That'll be pink eye . . . Have you been playing with that Taulson boy? He had pinkeye just this past week . . . Always sticking his fingers in his eyes and nose. That boy'll blind himself! Children these days . . . always fidgeting . . . always moving about . . .

—Can I have some medicine?

—Yes . . . Children . . . Children . . . We throw you out in the world and teach you nothing about the nature.

Nothing about germs . . . Never wash their hands . . . If it were up to me you wouldn't be allowed in the dining hall without putting your hands under a black light. I'd find the stragglers, too! They'd be made an example of! Do You wash your hands? You better or you'll be dead! You'll get Necrotizing Fasciitis! . . . the medicine . . . where's that medicine? Here! You'll have to stay here until you aren't contagious . . . pink eyes is incredibly infective. You know if they would get you children into bed early instead of going out and sitting out in the woods for hours on end . . . You need rest . . . that's why you're sick now is because you've probably been gallivanting about instead of resting . . . I'll have Mr. Natasha bring some of your things and you'll have to stay here all day . . . can't be too careful with pink eye. Goodness knows we don't want an epidemic! Then it'll be thirty of you in here . . . or more! We'll have to close the camp!

—What should I do now?

—Wash your hands!! With soap . . . and water! Hot water! I don't want pink eye. No, no, no. There's a VCR and a portable television in the storeroom. We've got quite the collection of Disney movies, goodness knows we need more of those. Pardon me. I've got some review tapes of first-aid techniques . . . quite interesting actually . . .

—Okay.

Nurse Rosa rolled a large television on a trolley into the bunk room I'd be staying in. The room was perfectly square with a flickering halogen light fixed to the ceiling accompanied by the faint smell of disinfectant. I sat on the bed and watched as Nurse Rosa plugged in the trolley then placed several drops of liquid into my eyes. She showed me how to use the remote then walked out of the room. I could hear her, minutes later, talking on the phone discussing the day's health incidents with concerned, or unconcerned, parents. I looked through the films trying to make a choice. I finally came upon one about suturing techniques. I picked this only because it looked gruesome and it'd give me an interesting story to share with the guys. It was one of those films with bright fonts and matter of fact hyperbolic voices.

As I watched the film, my eyes began to itch more and more. Little droplets of liquid leaked from them like a sinister oil. After getting through the film, I could no longer bear the state of them and went to the bathroom to get a moist paper towel to place over my eyes. In the bathroom the strumming of a guitar wafted through the walls, figuring it was coming from Nurse Rosa's office, I listened as I moistened the brown paper then walked back into the main room. As I walked past the pedestal holding the open manual the strumming grew louder as though the music were coming from the book itself. Laughing, I dismissed this notion as the meanderings of my imagination and continued back into the bunk room and laid on the vinyl mattress with the compress over my eyes and listened to the melodious rifts from the unseen instrument.

As I listened, I drifted to sleep and then dreaming. My eyes were cast above me in a kind of cloud. I watched as I awoke in the dream to a strange feeling in my stomach. I looked down to see a black, wriggling spine sticking from my stomach. It grew in length as other spines just like it started to burrow out in a similar fashion. I looked down as my seemingly pregnant stomach expanded. With each passing moment, the spines turned into giant insectoid legs hitting the shield of the halogen bulb. Suddenly my stomach burst! A head with eight beady black eyes poked out as if from a foxhole peering about the room with agitated quickness. The spider stood as big as the room and worse it seemed to have my consciousness. I walked on the spindly legs as I tried to come to grips with my situation. Suddenly a sound erupted below my feet causing the ground to shake. A great arm thrust through the ceiling grabbing me by the head. The veins seemed to sliver under the skin like ivy to Victorian buildings. The hand had long pointed nails with earth caught beneath them. It thrust me upward into the sky until I could scarcely make out the fine detail of trees then thrust me beneath the earth through miles of dirt into a large fiery chamber. The arm was connected to a face that I couldn't quite make out. It was obscured in a whirling mask of smoke. The arm dangled me before an open pit alive with fire. As I descended, my spindly legs curled before the heat. Finally a white face emerged from the flames with a great heap of hair and a long tattered beard. The terrible black eyes looked upon me with a terrible spite that burned greater than the fire devouring my legs. Finally, the hand let loose my ravaged body. Maniacal laughter filled the chamber as I was claimed by the fire. More than fire, the face emerging was far more frightening I awoke in the room. wondering at first where I was. My brain hovered in a haze of abandon. The faint humming of the halogen and Nurse Rosa's voice waging on in the distance seemed like far-gone sounds of a land submerged beneath leagues of ocean brine.

—Mrs. Zabina? Mrs. Zabina . . . Hello! Yes, this is Melody Rosa. Yes, camp nurse at Wannapayke. I was wondering if you could tell me what Danny eats on a regular basis at home? He hasn't been eating much and we always get concerned that these children will get worn out from lack of nourishment . . . Okay . . . Yes? . . . Oh, really? Hmmmmm . . . Peanut butter and jelly . . . Whatever pays the gas bill . . .

I was sweating badly as though a heavy blanket were wrapped around me. Fever. The itching of my eyes had transcended their boundary and had set my skin ablaze with red spots with two heavy welts dressing the top of my forehead. Such pressure building beneath them like submarines unable to break through crusts of Arctic ice. I jumped out of the bed itching my skin stumbling into the waiting room the pedestal was alive with action as the pages turned as if from a heavy wind. A dull light as if it were reflecting off of tin armor flashed a strange light from within glinting across the cross. As the pages turned they decried their subject: abrasions, burns, concussions, contusions, lacerations, compound bone fractures, brittle bone fractures, insomnia, sleepwalking, punctures. The golem bookcase creaked then exploded with a bang causing pages to whirl about the room . . . then all was still. I felt as if I'd witnessed some sort of sign. Nurse Rosa continued her conversation. The book upon the pedestal glowed brightly for a moment then dimmed. Soft music, coming from the pages, filled the room as though an orchestra of guitars had assembled in some hidden room. The notes as they hummed warmly made quick strides up and down the hidden necks. First slow with care to entice the listener, then faster and faster. The vibrations kicked back and forth echoing the chaos of the paper strewn room. I looked upon the slightly glowing volume splayed open upon the pedestal and dismissed the ramblings of my imagination realizing the truth of my previous dismissal. "Brain scurvy, man" recited my memory of Taulson's doubt. With this thought, the notes shifted into minor chords weaving a macabre hymn of welcomed darkness. Hallucinations! Faster and faster, the sounds of the guitar incensed me in unfathomable ecstasy as my skin entered a new wave of discomfort while at the same time becoming more and more enamored with the music. My mind begged for the music like an addict to his most darling drug! I wanted to be the master of this sound! I writhed with the growing draught of the guitar as I fell to the floor and began to seize. Natasha entered the room with my backpack and pillow as my dance on the floor lessened into minor jerks then stillness.

—Rosa! Rosa! Edwards' having some type of reaction!

—What? What did you call me?!

—NURSE Rosa!

—Goodness! Let's get him back to bed . . . feverish . . . Edwards? Edwards?!

—Yeah . . . Did you hear the music?

—Have you had the Chicken Pox?

—It was great . . . Where's the guitar . . .?

—You're delusional. You may have to go home . . . I'll call your mother. Parents leave their children inside too much. You should have had these ages ago. Well don't itch . . . you'll get scars . . .

They helped me to bed. Nurse Rosa applied a cool rag to my forehead then took my temperature.

—02 . . . Well, it's not the worst thing that could happen . . . but you're burning up . . . any higher and your mother will have to come and pick you up. Just take a rest. Ok?

I was groggy and going in and out of a kind of vertigo as I felt myself falling down through the bed into a pit. I drifted until I heard Nurse Rosa's voice coming from the other room. I heard the music again. It lulled me into a kind of stupor as it played slow melodic rhythms.

—He's progressing nicely. He'll be ready soon . . . of course. It'll be perfect . . . so perfect . . . We've placed him there with them . . . Yes . . . at Firebow—

She wasn't in her office but in the main room. Through the wall I sensed her voice coming from the direction of the pedestal as though she were speaking or reading from the book. I heard the words but could do nothing. The music's hypnotic melody paralyzed me leaving me at the mercy of an invisible will. My limbs hung like lead and my mind swarmed with static. The bunkroom seemed to contract and expand as though it were breathing becoming more and more animate with every passing hour. The halogen light breathed and coughed above me as the television trolley rolled about the room growling with my every movement! The screen flashed with static faces and great dilated eyes. The chaotic storm of faces gnashed with decayed teeth that took great gulps of my volition. Terror would have enveloped me if not for the quick strikes of muted strings that kept me docile to the bestial appliances. As the day progressed, I heard other voices entering and exiting the Infirmary. Taulson's voice pierced the walls of my demented prison in the late afternoon.

—How's he coming?

—The Master's guitar is taking its course. He's been out of it for most of the day and will be until we can get him to Firebowl. I'll summon the instrument in a few hours' time. That'll put everyone one else in motion. Make sure you wear your earplugs or you'll be just like him strung out and impotent.

—Will do.

After Taulson had left, I heard the door open again. Phil's voice echoed from outside of the screen door.

—Can I use the bathroom in here?

—No, use the bathhouse.

—But there's no soap in there and I have to do a 2.

—Fine! But don't make too much sound Edwards is ill and is trying to rest.

—Alrighty!

I could hear Phil walk towards the bathroom then stop. I imagined him looking about with exaggerated movements then tip toeing towards my door. Finally he entered and kneeled at my side. He looked upon me with surprise not expecting my pitiful state.

—You're really sick, Jon . . .

—No . . . they've done something to me . . . can you hear the music . . .?

—No . . . what are they doing to you?

—The book! The eyes! It's magic or something . . . they're preparing me for something at Firebowl tonight . . . If you hear music you have to plug your ears somehow. I tried earlier with the blanket but I could still hear it as clear as if it were playing inside of my head. Cover your ears if you hear anything out of the ordinary . . . and I think that Taulson has something to do with it. He was in here and knew that something was going on . . . and the shirt, man . . . ahhh . . .

—Taulson?! He wouldn't!

—I know, but he was just in here and he sounds like he's helping them. Be careful of him. Do you have your earplugs?

—Yeah, I grabbed them from the pool earlier. Do you think we'll still go on the night swim that Mr. Natasha promised?

—Doubt it. Put them in and don't take them out.

With that, Phil stood up and left. He hadn't wanted to go but I told him that Rosa would be checking on me soon and that if she caught him in here with me that he'd probably end up in a similar state. He stood up and molded the plugs into his ears and left. The guitar music had become more aggressive and was making it difficult to stay coherent. Hours passed as the melodious sound completely subdued me. To open my eyes was too great a task. I heard footsteps in the waiting room. They moved slowly over the floor towards the book on the pedestal. A voice was whispering outside the door but I couldn't hear as the music in my head had grown louder. I heard Nurse Rosa begin to sing a kind of sad song with a heavy twang. She sang the song until the guitar playing began to accompany her. She picked up speed and with her the guitar followed. The music stopped without even the whisper of another vibration. I heard the sound of a hollowed wooden body dropped onto the floor. I gathered the last of my strength and ran from the bunk room. Nurse Rosa seeing me held a non-varnished deep blond guitar in her arms with a length of twine for a strap. Seeing me, she swung the guitar and connected with the back of my head leaving the guitar intact and me lying motionless on the floor muttering as the pain swept over my body. Rosa picked me up and led me to the bunk room then locked the door from the outside. Moments later I heard the screen door open then the strumming of the guitar. Unlike the music in my head this was coming from above me, perhaps, on the roof. The movement of Nurse Rosa's fingers echoed loudly reverberating through the Birch trees infecting them with the melodious sound. As it moved through the trees, screams began to pepper the surrounding woods. Scream after scream. The screams moved closer to the Infirmary as Rosa's fingers repeated the macabre tune.

The door to the bunkroom opened casting a sliver of light over my face. Mr. Natasha crept into the room and picked me up and placed me over his shoulder. We walked back through the waiting room where the book glowed with dim light. As we exited the infirmary, I saw as Nurse Rosa approached the pedestal picking up the first-aid manual then wrapping it in a blanket. The guitar slung over her shoulder, she walked out locking the door behind her. Mr. Natasha placed me in the back of an elderly golf cart as he and Nurse Rosa took places in the front. The energetic whir of the battery pushed the cart forward passing clumps of walking campers and staff. The silence of the trek to Firebowl hung with strange gravity. Tonight all that could be heard was the slight movement of gravel under the slow haunt of bewitched feet. As the trees blurred into a hazy mask of gray, the White Face looked upon me from above with longing. The sun set as the cart moved faster and faster like a hound in pursuit of game. Past the cow pastures past the fields of grass. The kingdom of rocks on the trail crushed in the mad dash of the cart racing to the clearing. As we came to a stop, I looked up and saw the cross blooming with a halo of fire. Natasha got out of the cart and supervised the cabins as they took their seats on the long benches. Nurse Rosa had set the blanket bound manual on a stump near the cross, whispering words under her breath. Taulson stood behind the fire looking at me with the shadow of the fire stealing across his face. Rosa handed him the guitar which he began to play. His fingers danced over the frets with great efficiency causing the fire to grow in volume. Natasha lifted me and set me on a bench next to Nurse Rosa who'd taken a seat in the front. Natasha began to speak . . .

—Good evening, campers! How has your day been? Good, I hope! I wanted to take this time to discuss our friend, Jon E. Jon has become sick and needs our help to get better. He needs the help of our Lord . . . Let us commend Jon to these cleansing flames.

Nurse Rosa had made a cross on my forehead with a red liquid thick with grit. She was whispering to herself as Taulson pealed the blanket from me like a scab from unhealed skin. I tried to get away but he pushed me to the ground then kicked me hard in the ribs leaving me sputtering. Phil looked down from a seat on the opposite side of where I sat. His face was alight with concern dissimilar from the rest of the people who stared at the fire with placid faces their eyes not moving, not closing.

—Cast out by his creator! Left to sit in desolation! Bound by fate to test the souls of man! Well, now is the time to bind ourselves with his awesome power! Rosa! Bring the book!

—*Nurse* Rosa!

Nurse Rosa brought forth the book and held it high above her head. Taulson and Natasha carried me to a place before the fire with the care given only to the newest initiates of life. I shivered as a deep and penetrating chill spilled from my chest into my appendages. Nurse Rosa, with a great scream, threw the book into the fire. Taulson took the guitar played a quick rift then followed suit throwing the guitar in alongside the book. The muted cry of the breaking strings accompanied the eruption of the fire into a large pillar. Something stirred within me. Phil seemed shocked at the events taking place and ran to try and help me but to no avail. Taulson anticipated his movement and pushed him into the tendrils of the great pillar. His face, alight with surprise, would never change from that moment. His screams, ravenous for freedom, died away as the flames claimed all that was Phil. Regret and pain bloomed within me, though its tenure was short-lived as joy replaced it. I lifted myself from the ground as my strength increased. Ageless confidence filled me. The boy, dear John, ebbed away like a fractured shadow from explosive light. A quiet eulogy hung with the wood smoke as the memories of ruckus songs passed into the void of the departed. The rows of people stared upon me, their faces calm and waiting.

—We've been saved.

The Deer
Giulia Genevieve Pink

It was snowing sheets, and school was canceled. Dad stayed home to plow our driveway and the neighbors', intermittently coming back into the house to warm his rough palms by the fireplace. He stomped great puffs of snow by the front door welcome mat and shook the powder from the creases of his work pants before he sat down at the breakfast table beside me. He wore a plaid fleece zip-up with a cartoon of Pluto that his mother had embroidered. Pluto's eyes were different sizes, like he was drunk or trying to hold in a laugh.

Mom made me a cup of cocoa with the morning eggs. She put a spoonful of the powder in Dad's coffee and stirred it while she cleared her throat once, twice, then three times. She was about to ask for something that Dad wouldn't like.

"Lesley's going through a divorce," she stated mechanically. She tapped the cocoa spoon against Dad's mug and set the steaming cup in front of him on a crocheted potholder—another of Grandma's creations. "She could really use some time out of the house, and it would do Brenda and Allison some good, too. I'm going to invite them here for the day. The girls can skate on the pond and I'll talk with Lesley."

I'd met Lesley once a few months before when Mom hosted a Tupperware party. She had eyes like Mom's: kind and accommodating, though one had a green twinge around it, the kind from a bruise that looks uglier and uglier the more it heals.

Dad raised his thick eyebrows over the paper. They looked like expressive dancing caterpillars.

"I thought Keller moved out," the voice behind the paper said. He reached for his coffee and turned the hairy black caterpillars to Mom, who was busy with the toaster.

"You know how it's been. If this gets much worse, I think I may set up the front room for Lesley and the girls. Just for a week or two. Until he's really, really gone." Mom winced.

The day those girls and their mother came over, it was snowing cotton balls. My mother bundled me into a purple coat that a giraffe had drooled on the weekend before at the circus, and I wore a crocheted hat from Grandma that left tiny spots on my ears to go cold.

Allison was my age and had a snotty nose from hay fever and breath that smelled like celery. Brenda was twelve and moody. She was like an abused filly, hiding behind a cut of bangs and the hood of her sweatshirt—tasskittish when you moved too fast, and quick to bite.

We were sent out to the pond while my mother and their mother started tea. Allison slid on her stomach to the other end of the pond.

Brenda glided after her, her hands shoved into her pockets and her head scrunched into her shoulders against the chill.

I caught a snowflake in my mouth.

Allison let out a sudden shriek from the other end of the pond, and I took short slides out toward her and Brenda.

"Etta! It's dead!"

Brenda knelt by a mound of snow. She began brushing it off.

We all peered down into the clear ice. The deer's eyes were open, but not yet cloudy like other dead animals I'd seen. Its pink tongue peeked out.

Brenda made a sound that rang high from the back of her throat. Allison sniffed a line of clear snot back into her nose.

"We should say a few words for it and gather some flowers. It should be put to rest," Brenda said after a moment.

I slid over to the end of the pond by the bird feeders and began to pick fistfuls of brown and brittle cattails.

Brenda took the bunches from me and tied them with the brown leaves that shot out from the plants.

Allison traced RIP in the fluffy snow behind the deer. Brenda framed the deer with the cattail bundles. I patted the hump of its side. The short bristly hairs blew in the chilly wind.

Brenda said a short prayer, and we sat in silence. The snap of a branch in the thicket behind the deer rang out. The lot of us gasped and held our breath. A few moments passed, and the only sound was the phlegmy bubbling in Allison's throat as she breathed. We sat cold and aching on the ice until Brenda stood. "It was probably a rabbit," she said. We climbed up the yard back to the house.

Brenda patted my head when we reached the porch. "Will you look out for the deer? It will be stuck in the ice for a while."

"I don't think it can be lonely, Brenda."

She played with a hole in the finger of her glove. "Yes. I guess that's right."

The next day, Mom got a phone call from Lesley. She twirled and twirled the springy phone cord around her finger, said "Mhm, mhm," and hung up. Then she went into the front room and shut the door.

I sat at the breakfast table, forming a mound of clay into a lumpy dinosaur. Mom didn't come out when the dinosaur was finished, or the submarine after that, or the deer. I squashed the deer. She didn't come out, even when Dad came home.

He stamped the snow from his boots and frowned at the closed front room door. Then he pulled a large pot from the cupboard and began to stir up a goulash. He spooned a serving into a bowl and set it in front of me.

"Dad?"

"Yes."

The goulash was spicy. I poked a noodle and wiggled it on the end of my fork.

"When will mom come out?"

Dad cleared the stove and ladled out two more servings. He had a TV tray tucked carefully under one arm.

"I'm going in."

He padded down the hall and coaxed Mom to open the door. It latched behind him, and the creak of the TV tray unfolding followed. Shortly after, I heard a burst of giggles.

I finished my bowl. Game show music floated beneath the crack of the front room door, and I pictured Mom resting her head on Dad's chest, her slippered feet up on the ottoman, like how I lay on her when I'm sick and home from school.

I walked to the living room and looked out to the pond. The dusk had painted the sky pink and gray, and I strained to find the bristly hump of the deer among the long shadows that fell across the lawn. A spindly, four-legged outline stood at the far end of the pond. I grabbed a flashlight from the fireplace mantle and shone the beam out to light up the yard. Next to the dead drowned deer, a doe stood, gentle and brown. Stunned by the sudden light, she rushed into the thicket of weeds and pine trees with a mist of white snow at her hooves.

The Promise
Andrea Stepchuk

"Riverside?" After naming the place, images from the many stories we had listened to about the dreaded plantation flashed across the features of my younger sister, Kaylie's face. I wrapped my left arm around her.

"Don't you worry about Riverside." I attempted to soothe her one night. "You won't ever have to be scared of goin' there. I promise." Oh, those words that so easily slipped off of my tongue. I reflect on them now and regret ever uttering them. I wish I could snatch the words out of the air and stuff them back into my mouth. I long to lock them inside of me, because they are a lie. She would be scared. I would be scared.

The sun was a big ball of yellow rays rolling up the sky in Chester County, South Carolina. The day was July 15, 1851. My sister Kaylie was only ten years old and I fifteen. I remember the scorching heat and the smell of the rich soil drifting through the open window as it mixed with the delicious scent of the flapjacks and sizzling sausage we had prepared for breakfast. We labored quietly and efficiently that morning, finishing our chores quickly. We were slaves from birth, destined to forever submit to Miss Abigail Larson, the lady of the house. I never thought I would leave . . . until July 15, that is.

Miss Abigail was unusually stoic at breakfast. I quickly assumed we must have done something wrong by the way she eyed Kaylie and me suspiciously. I saw a complaint on her lips, just waiting to be formed into words and spill out of her mouth.

"I have a necklace," she began. "Perhaps you two know of it. It is a silver locket, with photos of my mother and father inside. I did not see it on my vanity this morning. Has either of you happened upon it? It is very valuable, monetarily and sentimentally. Whoever took it will be sold to Riverside, like the girl yesterday was. I don't tolerate stealing." Her sentences were punctuated distinctly and harshly. Her green eyes turned to slits as she scanned over Kaylie and me as if she were a vulture scanning her prey. Miss Abigail was not as cruel as Mr. Thornton at Riverside, but I was still scared of her.

"I'm sorry, Ma'am. We'll be sure to tell you if'n we see it," I offered kindly. I glanced at Kaylie as she began to stack the dishes on the table and carry them back to be washed. Her small hands shook, and her eyes flitted nervously between Miss Abigail and me. What could possibly have gotten her trembling all over like that? I nodded to Miss Abigail, grabbed a few plates of flapjacks off of the table, and hurriedly followed Kaylie to the kitchen.

"Kaylie, what's goin' on?" I inquired plainly. "You ain't actin' yerself at all. Last night you were quiet and today yer shakin' like you's got the fevuh!" I

80

tried to keep my tone down, but fear cinched my heart tightly, making it difficult to remain calm.

"I did it, Lydia," she began exasperatedly. "I took the locket! It was just so pretty! I went out to the fields. I was gonna take it back after wearin' it fer just a bit, but then it fell off my neck an' I didn't know!" She was shivering all over now, and her eyes resembled big pools of dark fear. She didn't have the opportunity to finish.

"So you're the culprit," Miss Abigail spat from the doorway to the kitchen. She held her head up arrogantly. "Mr. Thornton from Riverside is coming today." The name "Riverside" carried a stench like burnt stew on a steamy afternoon. It wafted strangely in the air and when inhaled, a wave of nausea slammed into me, stealing my breath. "You will leave with him," Miss Abigail continued, "for a price of course. I don't tolerate stealing." I felt as though someone had shoved a sword right in my heart. The pain burned through me at the words that I would lose my sister. She and God were all I had left in this life. I wouldn't lose her. She would die at Riverside. I had heard the stories. Kaylie was too weak. I had to do something.

"You can't! She'll die, Miss! You jus' can't send her there!" I pleaded desperately. It was no use. Mr. Thornton arrived later that afternoon. Up until when he arrived, I spent every minute with Kaylie, telling her not to be afraid.

"We'll work this out. I won't let anything happen to you. I promise." She would look up at me with tears collecting in her deep brown eyes. I embraced her tightly.

"I c-can't lose you. I-I jus' can't," I stated in broken words due to unshed tears filling my eyes.

Miss Abigail explained the situation to Mr. Thornton. He seized Kaylie's upper arm. She winced in pain. I lunged at him, desperately trying to pry his hand off of Kaylie's arm.

"Stop, Suh! Please! Don't hurt her none! Don't take her away! She'll die if'n you do!" *Oh, God! What do I do?* I was scared and out of my mind.

"I'll go." Everyone was so silent I could only hear my heart racing. That moment I realized something I hadn't before: I would do anything, absolutely *anything* I could possibly do to keep my sister from being thrown into that wagon. They stared at me as my words dangled in the air between us.

"Take her away." Miss Abigail declared after nodding her consent, so I left. Kaylie wailed and screamed as I was shoved into the back of a horse-drawn wagon.

"Stop it! Jus' stop! I done it! I done an' took the necklace!" Kaylie slumped to the ground. Her heart-wrenching cries echoed across the dirt road separating us.

The last I saw of her, she was a tiny form in the distance, growing smaller and smaller.

"I'll see you again," I whispered to her just before they took me away. But I didn't promise.

Autumn
Grant Kammer

Autumn rolls in to the city with the first cool breeze of the summer. She wears a green dress and carries just a suitcase. She's moving into the city for a while. She's found my ad for a roommate. A train ride, a few blocks, and she makes herself at home in the room across from mine. We don't really talk a lot, even though she's late on rent.

Autumn buys a twin bed and doesn't leave it much. I hardly see her eat. Autumn smokes cigarettes on the porch and she teaches me how to inhale. I think she is a good roommate though we still don't talk a lot. She keeps her things tidy.

Her hair moves from bleach blonde to brunette, then later shows amber roots and lowlights. She's been wearing a lot of gray and black lately. I wonder where her green dress went.

I get embarrassed when I catch myself thinking that Autumn is a great roommate because she has still not paid rent. I know money is tight for her, but I am still caught off guard by her generosity. When I talk to her, she listens. When I tell her I love fruits, she brings me a trash bag filled with apples. The other night she brought in a stack of cold pizza. She shows me a side sweet like cider. But she seems sad lately and it worries me.

When Autumn's speaks, her voice has become quiet like the gentle twee of a fleeting bird call. She has become dry and brittle. She is visibly gaunt and wilting. Her eyes now carry larger bags than Autumn herself ever did. When I ask her what's wrong, she sighs and I can feel the chill of her breath. She has no answers.

Autumn borrows my clippers to shave her head. She needs a change. Afterwards, she tells me she hates her job. Turns out she works nights. She says it feels like every shift gets longer. I think that the days have seemed shorter since I met Autumn, but I don't tell her. Instead, Autumn and I commiserate about work.

Before long, Autumn tells me she quit her job. She says they wouldn't shut up about her hair. When I ask her what she'll do next, she isn't sure. She just said she knew the train lines, and that they're an easy way to go far. I ask her what she'll do for money. She just says, "whatever."

With a little help from friends I found her a job at a garden center, but right away she said she doesn't feel right there. I told her she needs a job, needs money, needs to pay rent and to stay here with me but she just says she never signed anything. She knows I can afford this place without her. I remind her she owes me money. And she calls me a fascist.

As a last resort, I tell her how I feel. And she reminds me I hardly know her, that she is a stranger in my home, and that her place in this world is bigger than my house. Her story is bigger than me. But she pities me trapped in my little world.

I can't leave my home. Everything I know is this city. All my friends and family live here. I work here. I grew up here. I need to stay.

But Autumn can't stay anywhere long. She needs to leave; it is her nature. And I try to understand.

I realize now that Autumn is so much more than the green dresses she wore when we first met. She is more than the sunshine in her smile. It isn't her voice like birdsong that tells her story. I see now that Autumn is beautiful because she is strong. She is brave. She is free.

When she leaves, I hope to remember I can change, even if my city doesn't.

Same Time Next Week
Heidi Ann Barson

It was a cold January evening and I lit the logs in the fireplace. It's not easy to do but I was determined as there was something very calming about the crackling of a real fire. This was a time in my life when I was at the crossroads. I was alone, emotionally alone. My life lacked clarity. I seemed to wallow in self-pity. I had recently divorced and had three children to raise. I had lived a sheltered life while married and the outside world was something to fear. I was married at eighteen and had a child already on the way when I was married. I hadn't even learned how to drive a car. I depended on my husband for everything. Now suddenly a divorce and whole new way of life. I eventually dozed off and then awoke to the morning sky.

I had gotten a job working as a banquet manager, I had never had a job prior to my divorce. This was a huge adjustment and I was grateful for my boss to take a risk and hire me with no experience. Thankfully, I put myself together and hurried to work, now one of the necessities of my life, and while hurriedly helping to set up a buffet in our small banquet room, I heard, "Marg! Marg! Is that you?" I looked at this man calling my name with some bewilderment. He exclaimed, "You don't know who I am, do you?" For a moment I was caught off guard. I replied. "Of course I know who you are, Greg." It had been thirteen years since I'd seen him. We had dated many many years before until the army took him away. By the time he was released from service and returned home I was married and expecting a child, so we never rekindled our relationship. I was holding a bowl or ranch dressing, wearing black pants a white button-down shirt and a black bowtie. This was not my most attractive moment and I began to feel self-conscious, he had known me when I was younger and before three kids. Wait, he was asking me to go for coffee. I was trying to understand why. I was awkward at this point, nervous and still holding a big bowl of Ranch dressing like it was a security blanket. I didn't feel attracted to him, so why so nervous I wondered. This was not a romantic encounter, but a great feeling of reviving a friendship, especially for someone as lonely as I was. I hoped this feeling that I can only identify as insecurity would dissipate. I wondered what kind of a fool I would be if I actually had stirrings for him, when I can barely muster a conversation to tell him, yes let's grab coffee.

It was a good thing I made it through coffee and we managed to rekindle a friendship. It was Greg who convinced me to join him for a meeting at "Parents without Partners," known as PWP. This was an organization that was meant to bring single women and men with children together. There were weekly meetings and dances where lonely middle-aged men and women got together to meet one another in the hopes that a relationship might blossom. While I wasn't feeling like a fashion model, I had begun to feel better about myself. I liked putting on makeup and I had discovered jeans. Oh my, I had discovered jeans. I now lived in them. I hadn't worn jeans once while I was married. My ex-husband liked dresses so I wore dresses all the time. Greg said there was a meeting this weekend and I had a new pair of Jordache jeans and was feeling sassy. *Look out, PWP Marjorie is coming in with a roar*—well in all reality is was a meow but I was coming!

It was at this dance where I met George. We were immediately attracted to one another. It was almost cinematic how we met. This particular dance was at a banquet hall, my banquet hall, the place I worked. I wasn't going to let that stop me, I had the night off and a new pair of Jordache's and a beautiful Angora ivory sweater. I felt like I glowed as when I walked in, at least a handful of men turned and stared at me. While I was becoming more secure in my own skin, I wasn't prepared for that kind of attention and I began to feel self-conscious again.

I quickly made my way to a table and sat down. It seemed almost like a high school dance in that men were standing in a group and women were standing together and the big open empty space was the dance floor. I made my way to the bar where they had beer and wine. I ordered an ice wine from one of the girls I managed. I said hello to Ericka and ordered my favorite wine. It was sweet and didn't taste much like alcohol as I never developed a taste for alcohol but this was like liquid candy. I began talking to Ericka. I was telling her that I liked the Motown theme of this party. She was younger and I do not think she had the same feelings about Motown music.

I could feel a male presence standing behind me. I grew very nervous and my mind was racing. Then Ericka asked me what my favorite Motown song was. I was snapped back to reality because that was easy—my favorite Motown song was "You've Really Got a Hold on Me" by the Miracles. I suddenly didn't feel anyone behind me, I could turn around and not feel self-conscious.

It wasn't but a few minutes later that a handsome man, dressed in jeans and a blue blazer, approached me and said *may I have this dance* and at that moment the song changed and "You've Really Got a Hold on Me" began to play. I was weak in the knees, I couldn't believe this. Had he been the manly presence behind me? Did he hear me say this and then ask the DJ to play my favorite song or was this just a romantically serendipitous moment? Either way I was trembling with anticipation for him to hold me and dance this song with me.

He led me to the dance floor. He wasn't really tall, he wasn't a hunk. He wore glasses and was just a bit taller than me, but he was assertive and confident when he led me to the dance floor. That was it, I was on my way to the dance floor when I saw two women whispering and laughing. I wanted to feel self-conscious but something about George made me feel poised and self-assured. I hadn't felt like this before. We swayed slowly, rhythmically to "You've Really Got a Hold on Me." It was as if it were only him and I, and I was lovesick.

I became very popular with the men and hated by the women, as George's affections were centered on me. We were together at these dances then we began to see each other outside of PWP events. The women all wanted George, not because of his good looks but because of his wealth and his gorgeous house. I knew this because whenever the women would speak of George, their conversations were always about his home, his job, and his money! I grew uncomfortable at the PWP meetings as the women became caddy, talking about my hair, my looks, and my clothes. I felt strong when I was with him and he told me that he didn't want me to suffer being uncomfortable because the women were jealous of me. He said my beauty was why these women talked about me. He said that we should spend our time together privately.

We began to spend time at his house, no surprise. I felt out of place at his house as I lived in a small Detroit home and I drove a ten-year-old car while raising three children. I worked long hours as a banquet manager at the Danish Club while George was an intelligent man with a degree in engineering. He worked as an executive at a major steel company. I often wondered what he saw in me and anytime those thoughts would creep out he would quickly put my mind at ease telling how beautiful I was. He would call me his Marilyn Monroe, he hadn't known that I secretly thought Marilyn Monroe was an amazingly beautiful woman, so this compliment really resonated with me.

George and I became more involved emotionally and physically. He had a way of making me feel as though I was as beautiful as Marilyn Monroe. In fact, he bought me the book of her life story. When he called me his Marilyn, I would be transported and thought I was living a dream. I felt a stirring in places that were not previously awakened, and this was intoxicating.

Meanwhile, as I was treated poorly by PWP, everyone seemed to resent that I had a committed relationship with George. I was never invited to any of the private parties that the members would have outside of the regular meetings and dances. George of course was invited to all of them. He had to be present at all regular meetings as he was the president, and this was putting a strain on our relationship. I wasn't invited and he didn't seem to think it was any big deal that he was going to these parties without me. Still when we were alone things were exquisite. He had a way of touching me that made me feel deeply loved. It was both physical and emotional which made our relationship intense.

We had wonderfully romantic dates. I wasn't used to going out to so many places. I was really a homebound introvert, dedicated to making my family happy, while I was married. However now that I had George in my life I was different, my life was different, and it was good. I loved concerts and we went to several in Ann Arbor during the summer. I think one of my favorites was the Joan Baez concert. We would sit on the lawn like star-struck lovers. Lovers that could never be, we just didn't know it at the time. Our relationship wasn't without complications, we both had obligations to our families. He had three daughters who were raised and away at college. I still had children at home. My mother had moved in with me after my husband left to help and she never left. I had bought a puppy for the kids to sooth the burn of their dad no longer living with us. I hadn't thought that through because I got 120-pound bull mastiff named Jax, he was an excitable, playful lap dog—a gigantic lapdog! There were many occasions where George would be pinned to my much lived on couch because of Jax. While my kids and I would think this was hysterical because George would become very stiff while Jax would lick his glasses off his face. We would eventually be able to get Jax off of him and George would laugh but say, he was glad he never had a pet. His house was very much like a museum—everything has a place and everything was very expensive. Our circumstances wouldn't make for an ideal blended family, or so George thought. In fact, I felt sometimes he thought we were more like the Adams Family than the Brady Bunch. This was disheartening as I was so happy when we were together.

It was Feb. 14, 1982, a Saturday night, and George and I had agreed to spend the evening with our kids. Well, basically it was his idea that we spend the evening with our kids! He said his daughter was home from college for the weekend, so he felt he should spend it with her. I was blissfully unaware that George may be lying to me. I called his house about 10 p.m. and his daughter answered and said her dad was out for the evening. I asked her if he had gone to Karen's party and she replied meekly, yes. I knew of Karen's Valentine's Day party as everyone from PWP was invited. Karen was one of the women who was really hot for George and who treated me badly. At one of the meetings, she made a reference to old cars, Detroit, and low-class people. She had a great job working as a business lawyer and was really good with words and disguised insults, and I was usually the target. Holding back my breakdown, I asked George's daughter to have her dad call me in the morning. I cried myself to sleep that night.

Sunday morning George called with an apology for lying. He tried to explain because of his position as president of PWP he felt it was necessary to attend the party. If this was the case, why didn't he ask me to go with him? This opened a flood of emotions and thoughts that were racing through my mind. I wondered if he was embarrassed of me or was he just an insensitive player whose sexual appetite would only be quenched by many women, or even worse the feeling that I am not worthy? My reply to his explanation was simple: our relationship was over. I could not nor would not be with a man I could not trust. I had already lived a life of lies, cheating, and alcohol, and

88

would not do it again. I decided I would forgive him but didn't feel like we could date. He begged me to remain friends, and I agreed. I am not sure where that inner strength came from. Maybe I was all cried out and had nothing left to give. George and I would share phone conversations, coffee, an occasional dinner and enjoyed sending letters to one another. Some would think it was strange but it was almost reassuring that George was still a part, albeit small part, of my life.

Less than six months later I began to date a wonderful man, Ron. He loved dogs and enjoyed my kids. I didn't experience the passion I had felt with George. Yet I felt a love that made me secure and it wasn't complicated. I married him after a year of dating. George continued to call and we infrequently would write letters to each other, now that I was married. George and my correspondence was affectionate, not sexual, warm and thoughtful. Somehow, I knew our lives would remain intertwined forever. I would never cheat on Ron; I loved him and his laid-back demeanor. I do not believe I ever saw him in anything but a plaid shirt and jeans. He was trustworthy and loved me for me. Ron knew of George and he wasn't worried at all. Another reason I loved him. Then suddenly my husband died a few years after our marriage.

I was once again lonely and alone. It was now five years since my husband's death. George and I hadn't seen each other in a very long time. It had been over a year since I had heard from George. He had met someone and I was moving to a new home. It was a rare occasion that I would go out but I felt compelled to go to a summer concert called Music Under the Stars with friends. I pulled on some jeans, put on a white tee-shirt, and was off to hear the music. The opening song was "You've Really Got a Hold on Me,"." I couldn't believe it. I began to look around. It instantly brought me back to that dance and our bodies pulled tightly together and the rhythmic swaying. I was transported back to a time where I was joyful. I jumped up and began to turn around I did a complete 360 looking for a glimpse of George. This would definitely be a place he would go. Then I saw him. He was walking toward me as if we had planned to meet there. Needless to say, I was happy to resume a relationship of sorts with George only after we stood in the park and danced as we had the first time we met, to what would now and forever be our song.

He would come over on a regular basis. His life was simple, he was single again, and his children were gone making lives of their own. My life, however, had become more complicated.

I still had my mother and now I had to care for her and my son and his girlfriend who had recently moved home with their new infant son. I wanted to be the carefree woman, George wanted me to be, but life happened and I wasn't alone, in fact I had a full house and still many responsibilities. This would be too much for our relationship to handle, I knew that as I knew him.

In a moment of heated passion, he asked me to walk away from it all and come live with him. I couldn't, it just didn't feel right to leave my mother in a home and my grandson, son and daughter in law who couldn't afford to live on their own. Needless to say, we split again and remained friends.

Our feelings for one another never changed only the circumstances we were bound by. It has been thirty years and we still see each other. He would always say to me "same time next week" when we saw each other frequently. The irony is he still says it to me whenever we see each other, "same time next week" even though we do not see each other weekly. My reply is always "of course!" Just recently he married and our visits are even less frequent. Again, our relationship isn't sexual, but it nevertheless is profound. He always feels compelled to tell me he did not want to be alone and knew I would not leave the family. I think of him often and when I do my heart beats faster and I begin to smile. All I can say is—*George, you've really got a hold on me!*

A Rose for Monica
Niikah Hatfield

I watch the day pass by in slow glimmers, the sun creeping in squares across the floor. Everything sits, still and not moving. Objects become passive observers of time. Why are humans forever moving, rushing from place to place, and yet these objects sit still and peaceful?

A child moving through the space would touch things but not disturb them. In their own simple way, they would be peaceful too, and the objects would have no need to change. Sunrise, moonrise, set. The things sit, waiting. They are peaceful enough within themselves; they don't need a quest to nirvana and eternal peace. They are at rest. Content.

If only we could be so.

James stands in the shadows of a streetlight, a cigarette drooping from his fingers. Damp wind swirls around his long coat and pulls the smoke away from his lips. It carries with it the hint of spring, but the snowbanks are still thick and heavy.

He watches a woman walk up the street, lugging a portfolio at her side and bending her slender head in the wind. As she nears, his heart flutters for a moment. Her short brown hair frames a milky face and petal lips that remind him of summertime. The urge to run across the street and help her jolts his body, but when he goes to move his feet are rooted to the sidewalk.

She climbs the stairs of the house across from him and disappears inside.

After a moment, a light comes on in the highest gable window and a shadow moves behind the glass. He stares at it in silence, his mind gone to places far away and the cigarette burning to a stub in his hand.

Monica sits in the empty space of her room and tries to mimic the things set out on the table before her. Stillness, mindlessness, emptiness.

A paintbrush hangs loosely in her hand.

The canvas spread out on the rug before her is blank, not even a stray hair adorning its surface. Her eyes lift to the teapot, the empty cup, the spoon. Something is missing, but she doesn't know what. The words of her professor ring in her ears.

"Try something different," he'd said, after gazing at the abstract lines and colors flowing across her last painting. "Maybe a still life. See what's really there and capture how the light falls across the objects. It might help you."

She sighs and lays aside the paintbrush. There is nothing natural in the hard lines of ceramic, nothing that sparks her interest in the cold metal of the spoon. She wants something raw, something exciting.

The squares of sun inch further across the room.

When we are young, we gather what we know from others, we listen to what they say is right or wrong and take it as the truth. We are a blank canvas, and the projections of others seep into who we are. We hold them close, clutching at any part of human identity.

Without them we are nothing, just atoms pulsing in empty space, shivering at a different frequency than the rest of the world.

But we have the awareness of self.

We know the beating of our heart, the look on our face, the consequence of our actions as ourselves.

James goes into the flower shop before he can change his mind. He stands in front of the overflowing buckets of lilies and carnations and daisies and orchids, and after a minute picks a single rose from the container in the corner.

The girls behind the counter wrap it in pink tissue paper and take down the address for West Oak Street. He leaves without filling in the personalized card; he doesn't look in the rearview mirror when he turns onto the street.

The girl charged with delivering the rose climbs the five flights of stairs, the vase balanced in her grasp. Her breath is labored when she reaches the top, and she waits a moment before knocking on the door.

Only silence emanates from behind the square of candied glass. She knocks again. A faint "I'm coming" echoes from the depths of the apartment.

A woman opens the door. She stands in pajamas and a tank top, her hair tousled and half covering her eyes.

"A rose," the delivery girl says. "For you."

Monica takes the vase. Her eyes are wide, half awake.

"Th . . . thank you," she says.

The girl's footsteps recede down the stairwell, and Monica stares at the flower. There is no note, nothing besides the generic tag from the flower shop. She takes it to the other room and sits in front of the blank canvas.

Soft velvety petals linger in the still air, sitting upon a collar of five leaves. The stem has been cleaned, but there is one thorn left. She reaches out, feels the sharpness under her finger, and pulls away.

Her gaze falls on the still life, and she sets the vase with the rest of the objects on the table.

She stares at it, and in a moment of boldness she lays the first stroke of red on the canvas. The colors flow easily now, the language between the paint and brush a fluid conversation. Even the subtle curve of the stem and the elegant shape of the blossom is enough to make the scene come alive.

As the world is transposed onto the canvas, she disappears from the awkwardness of social life, from the corners of classrooms where she sits like an electron outside of the nuclear cluster.

The world, it turns.

She paints until the wee hours of morning, when she stands at last and stretches her aching hands. At her feet, the painting still shivers with the dampness of life. Saturn hangs like a bright star outside her window.

Some days it feels like I am nothing. Why do I exist except for to wake, to sleep, to keep moving on? I want to have purpose, but there are no easy answers. Words rise in my throat, but I cannot say them, I cannot speak until something has changed. I twist my hands, pound at the air with my heart. Something, anything, to show that I am alive, that I am doing right, and I would be content.

But sometimes there is nothing.

James wanders the streets of the city, feeling overdressed in his long coat. He thinks about taking it off, but shivers at the idea of being so bare.

A shadow crosses the street in front of him, and his heart jumps when he realizes it is her. She has a painting tucked under her arm, and he catches a glimpse of hard lines and a splash of color on the canvas as she walks away. He tries to formulate the words, to tell her to come back, let me walk with you. But his mouth turns dry, and when he opens it to speak, no words come out.

She turns around the corner, and he stands there for a while in the gentle falling snow, ignoring the slow seep of water into his shoes.

Receptive
Benjamin Champagne

Ever since the stroke, I cannot communicate. I want to talk to my wife the way I used to. I want to whisper in her ears. Say something meaningful. A guy from the shop sits in his chair and twists his fingers repetitively like he is still on the line. He is in the doctor's office every other time I am there. We have the same issue, but it's not the same. He can still love his family. Change the channels wantonly as he may, there is no confusion in his eyes.

My wife looked at the dishes in the sink and spoke slowly to me. She thinks my aphasia renders me deaf. I know what she is saying. She is saying that she is stressed. It is more than the dishes in the sink. I should put them in the dishwasher. I should rinse them. I should cook a proper dinner like I used to. I tell her I will put them away after I run to the hardware store.

"The route to nutting and semblance is all clear. Sit back and rely on the cleaning." Dammit. Damn.

I don't know how long I can continue.

Sometimes I think it would be easier for everyone if I froze into eternity. I read it in a novel before all words became jumbled. The serenity of turning blue in a snow bank. Of course in the story, the man saved a child and found a reason to persist. I want to tell my wife she is the reason I persist. She stands at the banister while I put my shoes and coat on.

I kissed her cheek. "Eternity is here and forthwith shall be some timble. But passing reasons never contain." Another psychotic neologism. She records them in a notebook. It is out of love. She is writing my dictionary. She knows that I can drive just fine. There is no enunciation necessary at the stop sign.

There is nothing I need to purchase at the hardware store. It is familiar. I don't mistake three-fourths-inch wrenches. I browse. It keeps me from turning blue. The man behind the counter is the son of an old co-worker. I don't see him much these days. But his son was raised right. He saved over the years to live his dream of owning a business. He always used to tell me that you can't get rich working for someone else. All of my pension money goes to the doctor. My wife hasn't been on vacation since I retired. I think if I stared at the screws long enough, I'll come home. I'll grab her by the waist and I'll say, "I love you."

Along the Beach
Brandin Dahlstrom

Here we were, aimlessly walking, the humidity already thick. It was early, my thoughts still seeped with dreams and drink, but you thought a walk might do us good. I wanted to be back indoors, back on the cool leather of the couch, in my own space, but I followed slowly behind you. For a moment I lost myself to the swishing sound of sand beneath my feet. In the distance, a glob of gray appeared stationary on the shore.

It was butter-flied open, boney and pink, its blind eyes turned upward. A clean gash ran from its head along its scaly back to the tip of its tail. Its mouth moved widely across its sleek head and appeared to tilt shyly in the direction of its eyes. Its sides were tapered down, soaking in salt water. We plucked a few of the pearly bones for luck, we said, but they were brittle and broke quickly. So, we sat in the sand, closer to it and each other. Our bronzed skin sticky with sweat. We were afraid to move it again, for fear that it may disappear and so we decided to keep watch over it for the remainder of the day.

Hours must have passed when we woke, still huddled together next to where we had left it, but it had seemingly vanished with the nightfall. We rose slowly, looking in every direction for a trace of its presence. It was you who spotted it out in the open water, drifting away. We stood on the shore, hand in hand, and watched the beacon of white disappear into the horizon.

Let Me In
Anna Dunigan

Disoriented and drowsy, I stumbled from my room and into the empty hallway. It was quieter than it had ever been before, and I could feel the hairs on my arms standing up. I tried to steady myself by resting my hand against the cinderblock walls, willing the room to stop spinning. I thought I heard someone calling my name but couldn't seem to turn my head enough to look.

Suddenly, a loud crash came from further down the hall, and the doors slammed open. Tall figures cloaked in black with white masks began to fill in, a violent buzz taking over the air. They just stood there, staring at me, and my veins turned cold. I heard a deep, throaty cackle, and a warning siren began to blare. One of the figures took a step forward, separating themselves from the pack, and let out a snarl.

"Run," it howled, the voice deep, raspy, inhuman. I turned around and willed my legs to move, but it was as if they were made of concrete. I let out a small scream and my eyes darted around, desperately searching for an exit. The curving hall had no end in sight, but there was an open door not too far from me. I turned my head to see that the figures were making their way towards me, and I put every ounce of energy in moving.

The door led me to a large room that was dingy and wet, with fluorescent lighting that flickered. I panted, the adrenaline coursing through my veins making it hard to breathe, and saw a smaller, hidden room in the corner. I stumbled in and slammed the door shut behind me, locking it with a resounding click. Sliding down against the door, I landed in a puddle of what I hoped was water. The sirens outside got louder and louder, and I knew they were coming for me. I covered my mouth with my hand, attempting to muffle the sounds of my ragged breaths.

"I know you're in there; come out, come out, wherever you are!" the voice bellowed, and I struggled to not make a sound. My eyes began to sting, and I felt the tears stream down my cheeks. I knew this was it.

The monster began to throw its body against the door, causing my head to slam against it. I stifled a scream and used all of my leg strength to hold myself against the door. Demonic laughs followed as it came at me again, and again, and again. My legs began to shake and I started praying to God, any god, that my legs don't give out.

Then, there was silence. All I could hear was my heart pounding in my ears and my labored breaths, now slowing down. I wiped away my tears, black makeup covering my hands, and I stood up slowly.

I was shivering, the cold of the water I had been sitting in finally sinking into my bones, when a voice called out to me. "Chandler, it's time. Let me in." It was soft and angelic, causing relief to wash over me. I let out a shaky sigh and took a step towards the door but couldn't bring myself to unlock it. "You can trust me," the voice sang. "Unlock the door."

As if hypnotized, my hand reached out and twisted the lock, the metal retracting back into itself with a clink. I took a step back and the door opened slowly, the white light blinding me. I could barely make out the woman in front of me, whose hand outstretched towards me. I placed my stained hand in her palm and let her save me.

I was focusing on perfecting my eyeliner when I heard my dorm room open. Out of the corner of my eye, I saw Chandler stumbling into the hallway. I chuckled quietly and followed her out there, knowing she needed supervision. She stumbled through the hall slowly, holding herself up by her hand.

"Chandler, come back in the room before someone sees you!" She barely turned her head towards me, and I was about to call her name again, but a loud bang at the end of the hall caused me to jump. People dressed in all black with *Scream* masks came spilling through the doorway, clustering together. They just stood around, taking in the scene when they locked onto Chandler. I started laughing, a deep cackle escaping my lips, knowing her inebriated status would make this an easy prank. The person in the front of the group held up a small megaphone, and a shrill siren began to blare. Shaking my head, I walked back into my room to clean our mess.

"Run," one of the guys bellowed, and Chandler's screamed response echoed through the halls. I could tell by the sounds of footsteps hitting water that she ran into our always flooded bathroom to hide. I sighed and grabbed her mostly gone drink to dump down the drain.

I walked down the hall, taking the scene in. The masked figures were beating on doors and screaming at anyone that poked their heads out, causing an even mix of responses, from screaming to laughing. I gave them no reaction, so they left me alone.

"I know you're in there," someone from within the bathroom called out. "Come out, come out, wherever you are!" I stepped closer to see three huge guys huddled around a closed stall door, laughing and shoving each other roughly. I rolled my eyes and squeezed past them, following through on my mission to dispose of the evidence. As the clear liquid swam down the sink, I looked around to see if I could figure out where Chandler was hiding.

Suddenly, one of the boys body-slammed into the door, causing the other two to laugh like hyenas. I rolled my eyes as I threw away the plastic cup and heard a small, girlish squeak from behind the door. I pushed my way through the boys, listening to hear if Chandler was okay. It sounded like she was crying, and my stomach dropped.

"Could you guys pick on someone your own size? She's clearly had enough!" I hissed at them, and their laughter slowly died. The one who had been slamming into the door shrugged and led the other two out.

Most of the commotion in the hall had passed, the group of delinquents moving on to another hallway to torment, and I waited so she could calm down before I tried coaxing her out. I placed my hand on the doorknob and felt that it was locked.

"Chandler, it's time. Let me in," I said quietly, trying to be as soothing as possible. I heard her sigh and walk closer to the door. "You can trust me. Unlock the door." I was afraid she wasn't going to listen, but I heard the metal lock clink and I opened the door slowly. The harsh, florescent light flooded the dark room she barricaded herself in, and I was able to see the makeup stains on her cheeks and hands, and the way she was shivering. I stretched my arm out to her, and she gladly placed her wet hand in mine, allowing me to escort her to safety.

Beneath the Snow
Delia Lee

The snow continued to drift slowly as she swept the blue tiled kitchen floor. Father had laid it down at mother's request. She loved all the shades of blues and greens; they were all over the house as living reminders of her. The refrigerator droned its own harmony as she glanced out of the window again, looking for the familiar hunched shadow of her father to come over the hill. The snow had layered high enough to engulf the ankles and knees of whoever challenged through it. She watched as someone made their way down the road. His stride was taller than her father's and his coat was not as torn and equally patched with old age as his. At this she sadly sighed, knowing the man walking was not her father. She continued with her cleaning when she heard a knock at the door. She quickly brushed the dust off her skirt and fixed her stray curls into a neat bun. The man outside had made his way to her front door, and she hesitated to open it. He knocked softly again.

"Ms. Isabelle, please open up. It's me, Mr. Lyon,"

She opened the door as wide as the tense smile politely crafted by her lips.

"Hello, Mr. Lyon, what a pleasure to see you."

"Yes, you too," he smiled. She could see his hot breath condensing in the cold.

"I am sorry for your long trip, but my father said he would be meeting you in town."

He was dressed as she expected him to be, in the most elegant way possible. Mr. Lyon was not overly wealthy, but he was the most mysteriously well-known man in town. Observing him, she noticed the bottoms of his cloak and pants had fallen victim to the snow.

"I had hoped to meet him here instead. May I come in and wait for him?" he asked.

She stepped aside allowed him to enter, nervous of how long his stay would be and more so of when her father would arrive.

Mr. Lyon stepped inside and removed his shoes. As he walked on the wooden floors, she noticed his socks leaving wet prints behind him. She frowned, as she had just mopped there. The coffee table in the middle of the living room had been polished so finely Mr. Lyon thought he could see his reflection. The room smelled of clean linens, with a hint of the mild chemicals she had used to clean. He glanced back at her, noticing she was still standing by the front door.

She had not been alone with Mr. Lyon, or any man, without her father or another person present. She glanced up from her fingers at the nervous expression reflecting back at her from his face. The whispers of him in town described him as a gentleman, with deceptive motives. She didn't think her father's business with him was wise.

Smiling at one another, they each sat in silence. Mr. Lyon watched her, as she cupped her hands in her lap. She did not know what to say to the man sitting directly across from her to make him feel welcome. Her father was the one to initiate such things. He would welcome visitors into the house, make them feel comfortable over a cup of coffee and discuss the daily issues of life.

"Would you like some coffee?" she asked suddenly.

"Yes, thank you," he responded, failing to hide a smile.

She jumped from the couch and into the kitchen to prepare the coffee for her guest. As she pulled the coffee from the cupboard, she glanced out the window above the sink. The sky was growing dark with the approaching night as the hope of her father's return began to worry her. The winds had turned violent and the flakes appeared to be bigger since Mr. Lyon arrived. She noticed an oddly large object lying in what should have been the road leading to the house. Mr. Lyon's footprints had long been recovered, as if he had never come down that same road. At first, she assumed it to be something that had traveled in the wind. It lay black in the snow and looked still. Looking closer, she noticed it moved in an even more irregular fashion, clearly not an object, but something living. Straining to see clearly, she recognized the patching of her father's cloak. Her mother's blues and greens. He had forced his way home despite the stubbornness of the weather and had fallen victim to it.

Shocked and horrified, she ran out of the kitchen and through the front door.

"He's out there!" she shouted.

Mr. Lyon watched her as she ran out the front door. He followed after her, calling her to come back inside through the blinding snow.

Reaching him first, she brushed away the snow that began to settle over her father. He lay motionless with his eyes closed and rapid breaths leaving his chapped lips. Mr. Lyon knelt down to gently lift her father and help her carry him the rest of the way home.

"You're still so cold," she murmured softly as she comforted her father who lay in fresh clothes on the couch before the blazing fireplace. Mr. Lyon sat quietly on the opposite blue couch next to the window, taking orders to help aid her father when she gave them. She glanced at him, realizing how different he looked from when he first arrived. He sat taller and looked more uncomfortable than earlier.

The snow had finally ceased, leaving the air too bitter and the roads too hidden for travel. It was late when it was decided that Mr. Lyon would have to stay in the guest room. Being alone with him gave her an unexpected chill, shooting through her body so forceful she glanced to make sure all the windows were closed.

100

She left her father resting in front of the fire, under the quilt her mother made, as she guided Mr. Lyon to the guest room on the second floor. Mr. Lyon silently followed her up the stairs, sensing the tension rippling from her.

"I hope this room is suitable for you until morning," she said to him.

"It will do," he smiled back darkly.

"Good night," she said as she handed him clean sheets, a blanket and a pillow at the room's door. He simply nodded and glared at her wickedly as she walked back down the stairs.

Coming back into the room where her father lay, she could see him fighting in his sleep.

"Father, wake up!" she shouted at him, shaking him gently. She moved back when he swung at her with his crippled fists. She continued to shake him, until finally he looked up into her eyes, frantically searching them.

"It was so cold. He, he needed my help," he rambled.

"Hush, it was only a dream,"

"He wanted you. He said it was time. No, I said. No," he whispered. She frowned at him as he continued.

"He wants you," he repeated, "I told him he couldn't have you. He left me. My friend left me for dead."

A tear ran down his wrinkled cheek and he started to shake with anger, as if the same chill that ripped through her was now traveling through him. Glancing behind her, she saw the root of her father's anger, as he pointed to Mr. Lyon, the glimmers of the blazing fireplace dancing off of him.

A Clockwork Dragon
Gabi O.

The prince sat with his hands folded in his lap, eyes glittering, as she tried not to squirm. "You've won the contest," he all but purred.

They were sitting in a small, private room of the castle, dimly lit and cozy from the tapestries draped over stone walls. They seemed to be alone, but she knew there were enough guards stationed outside to flood the room in an instant if the royal so much as sneezed wrong. The opulence and invisible scrutiny were making her itch.

Dani scratched her head, hoping the collection potion stains on her work tunic weren't soiling the velvet upholstery. "Not much of a feat," she said, taking her time with the words. "Most of the entries were . . . not so original."

"That's one way to say it," he replied, lips curling upward.

The instructions had been simple: bring the second son of the king a gift he delighted in above all the others, and be granted one request from the prince himself. The contest was open to both nobles and common folk, though most of her neighbors had scoffed at the idea of entering. "You watch," they'd told her as she worked day and night on her entry. "Some slip of a foreigner with jewels in her braids will bring a trinket as costs more than his castle, and you'll have wasted your time."

She'd ignored them and kept working.

They had been half right: most of the nobles present had passed over creativity in favor of flagrant expense, and almost every entry was a heavy, decorative piece encrusted with stones that sparkled in the light.

They'd been wrong about her project.

She'd suspected as much, but it hadn't slowed her heartbeat when the moment of truth had come—when the prince had looked past all the gold and jewels and chosen her miniature mechanical dragon, walking across the castle floor with clockwork precision and dull metal wings held aloft.

It still felt surreal to be sitting here with actual royalty—even a royal who sometimes rode into town with a single guard, like a lesser noble.

"Now, what would you like as your reward?" the prince asked. "Something . . . personal, I assume, since you requested a private audience." He gave her an odd look, gaze burning intensely under half-lowered lashes.

In a flash of horrific clarity, she understood. "No! No, gods, not anything like that."

"Oh." The prince blinked, then slumped back with a sigh. "Thank the Old Ones. When you requested we *talk* privately, I thought—well. And it would have been within your rights as winner, but gods." He ran a hand through his hair.

"That's not what I'm after, I swear." Perhaps she ought to tell him she would never be particularly interested in *that*, anyway, even if he wasn't bad to look at—or perhaps he'd take it as a personal insult, as her would-be suitors in the town had over the years. "I only wanted to ask a question."

The prince's expression closed off once more. "Ah. That was the point of the contest, I suppose. Pair the spare son. Though I imagine Father thought it would be a nobler girl popping this *question*." He straightened his back and folded his hands once more. "But please, don't feel awkward on that account. I was only thinking aloud. Your question?"

"What the hell do you have against oak cores in automatons?"

Silence. Then: "What?"

"Don't pretend you misheard. I want an answer."

"Did someone tell you to ask that?" The prince narrowed his eyes. "The maker of your dragon?"

"No. I heard you talking about it to your guard one market day, but you walked off before I heard any more."

Dani glared, then remembered who she was glaring at and settled for a faint scowl. "And *I* am my dragon's maker, thank you very much."

His eyebrows shot up. "It worked better than anything I've watched our royal tinkers piece together."

"Your royal tinkers—begging your pardon—are idiots. I see those two at the stalls when they come into town for supplies. Couldn't pick out fresh wolfsbane if it reared up and bit them."

The prince laughed.

"You think I'm jesting? They've got no concept of a fair price, either— every stall doubles their rates at the sight of those fools and they don't bat an eye."

"No, I believe you," he said. "I'd suspected, after reading a little about automatons, that they weren't as expert as they claimed. But Father only hired them because I begged, and I doubt he'd hire any to replace them."

"Shame," she said. "But you still haven't answered my question. Why not oak?"

"The whole point of the core is to soak in the potions that make the automaton run, isn't it? Pine is much more absorbent."

"And what about when you want to turn the thing off, and the whole sodden core has to be removed? There's such a thing as too much absorption."

The prince leaned forward in his chair. "But too little, and the potions need to be reapplied constantly."

"Better than your mechanical creatures running amok for days if someone gets the potion mix wrong."

"Fair. But that shouldn't be your concern. It's a tinker's job to make the best machine he can, not compensate for what mistakes might be made."

"It's a poor tinker who gives no thought to the future of her creations. What's an automaton no one can use?"

"It's art. Beautiful."

"And *art* can't have a purpose?" She realized she was leaning in now, too, absorbed in their conversation and speaking too loudly for the small room. Faint embarrassment colored her ears. "Pardon. I sell home automatons, for cleaning and such. I have to make them safe enough for *nobles* to operate, and it's—not always easy."

The prince laughed again. "I understand completely." He glanced toward the door. "Though I suspect the guards won't appreciate your passion. They'll probably be in soon to investigate the ruckus."

Dani nodded and stood, avoiding his eyes. "I've got what I came here for, your highness. I hope you enjoy the dragon."

But the prince stood, too. "This may be a strange request, but—could I talk to you again? I've quite enjoyed our conversation, and no one else in the castle really cares for my technical talk. Or any other talk, with me."

She shrugged coolly as a warm sort of pleasure settled in her stomach. "If you'd like? No one I know listens about my work, either, so this was . . . nice." She thought for a moment. "I'm usually at my stall, if you'd like to come down next market day."

"I had something else in mind," the prince replied. "How would you like to be the new royal tinker?"

She blinked. "I thought the king wouldn't hire more tinkers."

"The king doesn't know your only request of me was an answer. We'll tell him you asked for a job, and he'll have to agree to it." The prince smiled at her. "What do you say?"

"Can I keep my usual stall?" She paused. "Will I have to work with those other fools?"

"No, I've wanted to fire them for years. And yes, of course you may."

Dani smiled. "Then, highness, you've got yourself a tinker."

Greener
Megan Locatis

Z had lived at the Spaceport for more years than she could remember. For her species—variant 1202G demi-humanoid, Bipedal Erectus, skin tone a pleasantly pale shade of purple for those alien races able to perceive color—a life spent in the sprawling quasi-bazaar was all that could be expected. Her parents, aunts, uncles, and cousins had been picking the streets for scrap metal and lost valuables ever since their generation had arrived en masse with her grandparents nearly half a century ago.

Unfortunately, a majority of them had died of exposure to an unauthorized permutation of cooling fluid that ran through the walls in their subsector of municipal housing. Z hadn't been around at the time, having decided, on the cusp of womanhood, that she was moving to the Green District of Blagua 7F, to make her own way. Her family had laughed at her upon her announcement, telling her that those streets were always picked clean before any of the planet's three suns were up, and that she'd never make a living there.

Z was convinced that none of them understood. The Yellow District was a slum, where the scrappers and second-hand hawkers congregated like twelve-legged roaches. The neo-fluorescent lights shone all night, drowning out the night sky in their orangish haze, and strange Cephalodean music—clicks, squalls, the occasional shriek—blared all night out the open window of surrounding housing complexes. It was a pit. A black hole. And Z was going to get away before she could be sucked in and crushed like the rest of them.

Sure, she didn't know what she would *do* in the Green District, but that was where the technomancers and gear wizards thrived, where the latest in off-planet gadgetry was set on display for passersby, where the savvy went to talk about Hi-Density R5 chips and the latest Triple Thunder 8.0Cablewire. That was where everything happened, where fortunes were made, where Credits were exchanged like dirty Ravlonar jokes.

She arrived without a job and an empty stomach, and she spent her first five days of the nine-day work week scraping garbage off the ground and sifting through it meticulously, hoping to come across any tiny techno-component that she could pawn off for a few Credits. The miniscule plastic chip she'd found with three wires—which she'd seen displayed at one or two stalls—was swapped for enough to buy a street gyro made with something that might have once been meat.

The fourth day saw her blessed. One of the vid screens on the building advertised the need for more janitors—municipally sponsored, housing included.

The very next day she was issued her official KleenKap and PPI—Personal Portable Incinerator. She would be paid based on the volume of trash she destroyed during the day. Her apartment key had been written into her ID code. And for the first time in her life, Z felt hopeful of the future that she was starting here, on her own.

She'd start small, trading in the rare treasures she stumbled across, socking away Credit after Credit, until she had enough to start buying when prices were good. She'd become a tech expert during her rounds, lingering by the stalls to overhear the professionals negotiating and describing their wares. Eventually she'd be able to enter the business on her own. She'd linger behind her stall, picking out cream-of-the-crop clientele, expertly pushing the latest and greatest on and cashing in on her very fair profit margins.

And eventually she'd have enough for a ticket out. She'd go somewhere nice. Sector XG8, or over toward the Traumar Galaxy. Word was that the Olmoron Federation that ran things there was fair-minded and knew how to keep the business climate favorable. Everyone and their interspecies half-brother was clamoring to get there, and get while the getting was good.

Her janitorial work, as it turned out, did not provide the steady income she'd initially imagined. At the end of her first day, when she'd plugged her machine into the nearest access port to receive her day's Credits, she was disheartened by the insignificant number that flashed on the screen. Scarcely enough for a cheap and questionable dinner from one of the street stalls, or maybe a nutrient paste packet from one of the Municipal vendor units.

So the next day she threw herself into her work, incinerating anything that she could find.

That night she barely had enough for a carton of steamed canal grubs. Her Credits flashed a red "0" on the screen. When she screamed at the unit that it couldn't possibly be right, that her incinerator was defective, that her trash volume wasn't registering, the unit processed her query and the helpful voice assistant returned with ten pages of fine print explaining fluctuations in fuel rate price, city waste management demand, etc., all which would affect her daily pay.

Selling trash, she quickly found, was more lucrative than burning it. Incinerating waste was something to do only enough to keep her municipal housing. She'd run across other janitors who'd told her the exact amount she needed to incinerate per week (.25 standard units' worth). The rest of the time she spent picking through piles of junk drenched in strange fluids that she hoped wouldn't eat through her skin. At first she watched the other pickers determine whether certain piles were safe or not. Eventually she was confident enough to leave the picked-over dumping grounds for secluded alleys and abandoned plots, where she rifled through foul-smelling oddities for her own pieces of lost treasure.

Most nights she went to sleep hungry, with nothing to her name but a faint hope that the next day would be better. Outside her apartment window, Nashorn disco-drumming echoed late into the night, overlaying the squabbling of two female Lokysians whose indignant shrilling could have shattered fortified Grade 86B Polyurethane-Reinforced Titanium. She began to think about the Red District, devoted to on-board weapons components and the like. It seemed like a better investment for her time. And it wasn't like she was particularly attached to the Green District anyway. The techno-industry seemed to be stalling, and the market was flooded.

It was three years before Fate smiled on her again.

It was lying tucked under a hefty piece of rusted scrap metal. It was an innocent-enough peach card, arrayed along the edges with glimmering little chips that caught the light from all three suns like dimondium crystals.

Z knew it by sight, though she'd never seen an MC card quite so fancy. Sometimes off-planet visitors would lose their preloaded cards, though there was never a significant amount left on them in Z's experience. But this little peach number felt different. Z ran straight to an access port to check the balance.

She nearly fainted dead away.

She had enough on that screen for a ticket to anywhere.

She finally had her break here, in her two hands. Enough money to leave. What if some slime-covered street spawn nicked it from her pocket while she was filling out termination papers through the access port?

No reason to chance it. She gripped her boon from the Universe and headed straight for the center of the Spaceport. At the Ticket Kiosk, she selected the first departure destined for the Olmoron-controlled Streichanax.

Z was hurtling toward the stars, out of anonymity and into greatness. In Streichanax she would start raking in—well, something. Whatever the Olmoronians used as currency these days. The long struggle was over. The hungry nights finished.

She stepped out into Starcraft Station and inhaled deeply. It was the scent of freedom.

Z hesitated. What now? There were probably too many possibilities to even process.

She watched the vids for a time, contemplating. And then she saw it, and she knew.

The next day she was a fully-inducted Starcraft Station Custodian, complete with her official Tidy Trilby and her IVU—Individual Vaporization Unit. Her new job even came with a Federation-sponsored flat in the Square District. Yes, things were definitely looking up.

Face the Demons—Just Not Your Own
Renée Beaudoin

A sad man in tattered shoes and a leather jacket two sizes too big eased himself onto the bench beside Tia. She fought back the impulse to glare at the man; instead, she stared straight ahead, refusing to acknowledge him. It was people like him—so visibly distraught and defeated—that brought her the greatest conflict.

A chime sounded overhead, high and clear over the chatter in the congested train station. A disembodied voice regretted to inform passengers of line B502 outbound to Los Angeles that there would be a fifteen-minute delay. Tia gritted her teeth and wrapped her arms tightly around her bulging carry-on suitcase. Fifteen more minutes? Next to *him*? Her fingers itched towards the eyepatch buried in the front pouch of the suitcase, but she stilled the movement. It was the first day in years she had gone out into public without the fabric over her left green eye, and she wasn't going to be spooked into putting it on just yet.

"Ma'am?" the sad man croaked. He cleared his throat. "Ma'am, what was that announcement? Something about the train to Las Vegas?"

"To L.A.," Tia replied curtly. She focused on a flashing ad across the room, the lights burning into her eyes.

"Oh." A moment of silence passed, then it seemed he felt compelled to explain. "Glad it's not Vegas. That's where I'm headin'."

Tia gave a grunt of acknowledgment.

Seeming to take the noise as an invitation, he went on. "Might have a job interview at a casino there. I could be makin' big buck in just a few weeks. That's what I need. Yeah, that's just what I need. A good-payin' job and—damn."

Something hit the ground with a *thunk* and rolled into her foot.

"Uh, sweetheart, can you—?"

Blinking spots out of her eyes, Tia reached down and grabbed the thermos. Hot liquid sloshed out of a crack in the lid and landed on her hand. She winced as she passed it back to him, and in that single moment, she met his gaze.

His cracked glasses perched on the edge of his pointed nose, his beady eyes widening in surprise as he registered her mismatched eyes. A bald patch illuminated the top of his head, crowned with long stringy hair. He tried to mask his stare with a toothy grin, and as he did so, his demons appeared one by one, masses of indescribable shapes and colors, convulsing and fuming around him.

The distorted figure of a bully she called Taunts struck out haphazardly at gray Grief as they flitted around each other. A frail child she knew as

Helplessness huddled between them. Hovering behind them all rose jittery Compulsion, desperately trying to grasp the air around it. One by one, those faceless beings turned towards Tia, sneering and crying out as they realized that she saw them.

Panic rose in her throat as a faint buzzing entered her head. She tried to focus on the man himself, but his demons surged forward, eager for her attention. Tia flinched instinctively as Helplessness clutched at her like it was drowning.

"You got really neat eyes, sweetheart. Green and brown—don't think I've seen that before."

Tia pulled back to the far side of the bench, forcing her gaze away. "Yup."

"Does it run in your family?"

She almost laughed. If it had run in her family, maybe her childhood would have been less of a nightmare. Her parents thought her eyes were strange, yes, but they didn't realize that it changed her vision—that it enabled her to see too much.

If it had run in Tia's family, maybe her parents wouldn't have ignored her when she told them about the monsters she saw at school. Her second grade teacher was shadowed daily by a faceless scary man that raised its fist and shrieked at her. When it realized Tia could see it, the demon would leer at her and grow more solid, and the teacher would become distracted. Tia named it Abuse, and to this day prayed that once she'd left the teacher's life, the demon's power had been diminished somewhat.

Tia had understood long ago that she if acknowledged the demons' existence, they exerted more control over their victim.

Hopelessness sidled into her line of vision, so she closed her eyes. The darkness was welcoming, but she knew that unless the man left, his demons would still be lurking when she opened them again.

Beside her, she felt Hopelessness squeeze between her and the man, pressing close against him. She could sense Grief breathing down their necks.

"I—I didn't mean to pry," he said sadly. "It's just—I haven't really talked to anyone for a while, you know? Ma was the only one I got and we took care of each other. I . . . I made things hard for her sometimes, sure, but she never got mad at me, not even when I went down to the casino and . . . Well." He spread his hands in defeat. "Vegas is the only idea I got left."

This wasn't working. Even with her eyes closed, Tia could feel the demons growing stronger. If she didn't end this conversation soon, they would begin to overwhelm him. And if he was already broken down, if they got too strong . . . It had happened only once before, but that was one death too many on her hands.

Her eyes flew open and she stood so abruptly she nearly knocked into a woman passing by. The woman glared at her, and the next moment was flanked by Self-Loathing and Suspicion. Tia quickly averted her eyes and focused on the man.

"I'm sorry about your mother," Tia said as sincerely as she could. "I hope Vegas is what you need it to be."

The man began to utter his thanks, but Tia was already moving, gripping her suitcase close as she propelled herself past travelers and earning angry glances. She kept her eyes trained on the sign for the restroom, trying not to excite the demons that were slowly manifesting around her.

She burst into the bathroom, bracing herself for more strange looks. Mercifully, it was empty. Tia let her suitcase clatter to the floor and she dropped to her knees, frantically digging for that damn eye patch. The odd-eyed ophthalmologist had "prescribed" it to her when she was ten, and it had always blocked the demons. Her fingers found the worn fabric and she stood, going to check the mirror as she put it on—Something was staring back at her.

She froze, eyepatch clutched in her hand, staring at the reflection that stood behind her. It had more form than any other demon she'd seen, and she had long suspected it was because of how familiar she was with it. At a glance, it looked like Tia, except its face was too animated, its body almost stark white, and the eyes a piercing, unforgiving green.

Tia's only demon met her gaze in the mirror. She thought that perhaps the demon looked disapproving, or regretful. Whatever it felt, Tia didn't care.

"Screw you, Knowledge," Tia hissed at her demon, before securing the eyepatch over her head.

She blinked rapidly to clear the vision in her right eye, and Knowledge was gone. Letting out a pent-up breath, Tia slouched against the wall, rubbing her eye as she resigned herself to wait in the bathroom until the train arrived to take her to Los Angeles.

Instincts
Madison Vassari

Her eyes fell heavy as she glided over the dark country road. The bright, sporadic glow of the moon punctured tree limbs and jarred her back from the temptation of sleep. A crooked brown sign emerged out of the darkness and ushered her into the night. Though the dashboard clock was faint, its pale green tint glowed with the pressure of every fleeting minute. So with a bare foot she pushed the pedal against the floor and the Volvo purred in return.

A soft moan rose from behind and she peered into the rearview mirror at the beads of sweat surfacing on the boy's forehead. The tree line broke suddenly and the moonlight illuminated her boy resting on the wool cushions. With the prominence of the moon highlighting his features and that panged look, she saw his father. She longed for the man who still lingered in the child's words and expressions. But her son was all that remained of the menace that came before—and still lurked within him. The tree line resumed and both faces disappeared under the shadow.

The road forked and she followed the one less paved. Her car crunched over stones and twigs and its rickety chassis stirred the sleeping boy. He clenched his stomach now and moaned something fierce. Under a colony of trembling aspens, a vacant parking lot greeted them. The hum of the Volvo's engine echoed past another brown sign that bade them welcome to PORCUPINE MOUNTAIN WILDERNESS STATE PARK.

"We're here, pumpkin."

He started pulling at his shirt and grinding his teeth. Whatever time she had left was sparse. There was no telling when he would start to seize. She pulled a lever and heard the *pop* of the Volvo's trunk detaching. Outside of the car, his moans were muffled, but his figure continued to struggle behind the windows. Inside the trunk was a neon-colored gym bag from which she pulled a spray bottle.

It was always best to start far away from the trails even though it was late enough that he would most likely not encounter any hikers. She started by spraying a yellow mist a few yards from the thick of the woods. The spray gave off a pungent smell that had her breathing through her mouth. She created a scented path from asphalt and gravel to branches and shrubs. Hopefully it was enough to point him toward game.

The car was still running when she returned, but inside was still and quiet. Her time was nearly spent; any more delay would lead to trouble. She swung the rear door open and began to loosen the laces of his shoes before slipping them off and tossing them to the floor. Then she rolled his snug corduroys down and peeled the socks from off his feet. His slender arms had to be guided through the pits of his shirt. She cradled his limp body and carried him from the car. There was a soft patch of leaves and grass where she set him down. As he lay there, he looked to her an angel worse for wear. His damp hair clung to his forehead and his soft breathing labored. Her hands stroked his hair and she gave him a kiss goodnight before striding back to her car.

The transmission creaked as she shifted into reverse and backed up, facing the entrance of the parking lot. The Volvo idled for a moment while she studied the stiff, tangled silhouette of her son in the dim red of her brake lights. She sighed away a fit of tears and peeled out of the lot. The loose gravel wailed against the car. He was in Nature's hands now, a Mother crueler than she could ever be, one to spite him with such a blight upon an otherwise kindly conscience. She was but a surrogate for this curse to continue.

She followed the road back to a rest stop populated by a few lonesome semi-trucks and a station wagon. Vending machines glared a chill blue hue through her windows, reminding her of a nightlight her mother had carved him: the wooden outline of a bear cub dangling from a tree while its mother reached up with great big paws, silhouetted by the warm glow of the bulb behind it. An old Willie Nelson cassette of *Always on My Mind* clicked on and she reclined her seat. This was usually how the night of her monthly ritual came to a close. Music drowned the guilt that personified itself as her child while she nursed herself to sleep with Nyquil. But on these nights she always slept best for reasons that ran and hid from her.

He starts school again in a couple of weeks. We haven't even gone back-to-school shopping.

When he ran toward the teachers and the kids on their first day of primary school, his oversized backpack flung up and down across his back. It made him look like such a little thing, his bag over-filled with anticipation. She chuckled at the recollection and brought a hand to her face, wiping away tears. Innocence was a comfort her son lost much too soon. They had already gone through more than half of their savings making the move out here.

It's worth it. I love seeing that kiddo smile. Does he still like those shoes that light up when you walk in them?

It was midnight. The moon swelled full and luminous in the mid-sky. Her son would be hunting for sustenance soon. Only it wasn't her son, but the foul pedigree he had the great misfortune of inheriting. The first light of dawn would wake her if for tonight the devil still refused to take her.

There was a thumping that echoed in the room. She was with her grandmother, knitting away by a fireplace in true-to-form Thomas Kinkade fashion. The thumping inspired the flames to jump from the hearth. They clung to her grandmother's knitting, consuming the yarn as it climbed up her arms. The thumping became sharper, and she woke to a man knocking on the driver's side window. His wedding band filled the Volvo with a shrill echo. She looked around the lot, deserted save for a Ford Taurus with its hood

112

propped. She combed her fingers through her hair and cranked the window down a few inches.

"I'm terribly sorry to wake you like this," he said. "But could I trouble you for a jump?"

She looked around the car. "I don't know where it is."

He lifted up a coil of cables. "I've got jumpers if you could just let me take some of your juice." He smiled.

The light of the dashboard clock ebbed dimly into vague digits. Whatever time it read, the sun was far higher than it should be. Her keys dangled in the ignition when she gripped them and twisted. The engine only stuttered and the man outside said, "You might need jumped yourself."

The clock flickered with the ambivalence of the engine and her face flushed with blood. She pressed the accelerator while she turned the keys again. The Volvo turned over with vigor.

"Look at that! All isn't lost," the stranger shouted over the motor.

The clock glowed just shy of seven o'clock and she grabbed the shifter.

The man outside knocked again. "Hey, wait. Aren't you going to help me?"

"I can't. I've got to be somewhere."

"Well, so do I! It'll only take a minute, please. There's nobody else around here."

She avoided his eyes as she pulled past the man by her window. These mornings left no room to alter routine and even then she was running later than she would have liked. He stood dumbfounded in the rearview mirror, the coil of cables strung about his feet.

The sun had already climbed above the horizon, casting a warm orange that faded into purples and blues. Morning commuters had yet to hit the road. Only a tractor piloted by an early-to-rise farmer crept before her. She passed him on the same country road that she navigated the night prior. Lonely farmhouses, weathered barns, and pastures of alpaca sprouted where nothing but darkness existed only hours before. The crooked sign appeared in the distance and welcomed her back.

Even the lot looked different in the light of day. She feared for a passing moment that she was there in error before noticing a patch of flattened grass and snapped tree branches. After parking the car close to the trail, she pulled the duffle bag from her trunk and slung it over her shoulder. From beneath her t-shirt she pulled a thin metal whistle looped with twine. She let it slack from her neck while she crouched to inspect the onset of his tracks.

The imprint of his little hand was pushed into the dirt. She traced the outline with her finger and tried to fit her own big hand into the crater of his. A few feet from his childlike traces were deep trenches clawed into the side of a birch. She held back tears, trying not to fathom the pain her boy had to endure after she left him. If it was anything like what made his father holler those guttural noises when the affliction came—but for a body so small to withstand as much. She continued along the newly born trail that months of relocating him had trained her to follow.

Usually she tracked him a few hundred feet before his markings became sparse and the gap in his tracks wide. This was when the whistle she wore with her at all times revealed its function. She would press her lips to it and blow until her breath expired. No matter how hard she pushed the air in her lungs through the narrow tunnel of the whistle, the sound emitted from it would always fall deaf on human ears. But to her son, the screeching note pierced throughout the thick of the woods and resonated in the expanse.

She'd lost his trail when she came upon the wrecked carcass of a doe. Its fur was glazed with its own blood and most of its belly was torn apart. Its lower innards lay discarded by its side. She knew her son's nocturnal habit, that instinct dictated he find shelter shortly after gorging. She looked around for any kind of makeshift shelter. A downed tree rested beyond the devoured deer and the pink of Eli's flesh contrasted with the rotting bark. She put the whistle to her lips, inhaled and blew only slightly through the chamber. His body jerked at the familiar pitch and he awoke groggy and inebriated.

His face was caked with blood and his tummy swollen. She bent down and unpackaged a wet wipe to clean around his lips and nose. From the duffle bag she pulled a fresh set of clothes and helped him into them. She was tying the laces of his boots when he said in his drowsy way, "Good morning, Mama."

She chuckled. "Good morning, pumpkin."

Lines
Shane Emery

My family lived in an old house, a little wooden box at the end of a gravel drive on a great wooded lot. The river marked one side and an expanse of farmland bordered the other. Across the dirt road, a larger wooden box stood out on a smooth lawn. This is where Tilia lived. She and I being of roughly the same age and the only two children who lived on Newman Road, we found ourselves friends.

There was a day, during the summer after my twelfth birthday, that began in my mother's garden. She kept it in a clearing among the trees around our house, filling it with flowers and vegetables. I would help her by watching my baby brother while she worked.

Sam was mostly easy to occupy. I simply needed to provide him with an assortment of objects and he would proceed to repeatedly throw them around and crawl after them. He also had a great fascination with bugs, and I had to keep a careful eye on him as he sought to pick up as many as he could from where they crawled on the ground.

Sam was in an uncharacteristically calm state on that day. He and I spent a good while watching the progress of a snail while my mother picked tomatoes. The snail had a bright shell, the color deepening with each turn of the spiral. It moved slowly: the pace of the bright morning.

Tilia arrived quietly, as she always did, her bare feet appearing at the edge of my vision. I looked up to find her beaming down at Sam and the snail. She edged forward carefully and lowered herself to the ground, pulling something gently from her pocket.

"Look, Sam," Tilia whispered, "I found a sleepy bee."

She unfurled a large leaf in her hand to reveal a small worker bee walking lazily across the leaf's veins. Sam giggled as Tilia helped him hold his hand still to let the bee crawl on. We all watched with wonder as the little creature made it onto the baby's wrist. Then, perhaps feeling the tickle of the tiny feet on his skin, Sam wriggled his arm and the bee took off, zigzagging across the yard. I smiled at Tilia.

"Wanna camp out tonight?" she asked, smiling back and pulling Sam into her lap.

"Sure," I said. "I just have to ask Mom."

"Hey, Mrs. Lines," Tilia called sweetly over to my mother, "It okay with you if Carly sleeps over tonight?"

"Long as it's okay with your folks, dear," my mother's voice came back.

"Sure is."

"Alright then."

"Sound good?" Tilia asked, turning back to me.

"Of course," I said, beaming.

"I'll see you later then. I gotta get back and help Mama."

"See you."

I watched Tilia wander back down the drive. Sam and I returned to our study of the snail, but he soon became restless, so I took him inside to start lunch. My mother followed soon after and then my father's truck came rolling up the drive, delivering him home early.

"What are you home for? I asked him as he came in the kitchen door.

"What, ain't you happy to see me?" he replied, pulling off his work boots, smiling.

"Yeah," I said, giggling.

"I gotta meet with Mr. Mason in a little bit."

"'Bout what?"

"Oh, he wants to take down some trees at the edge of the field. More room for his tractors or somethin'."

"Oh, I wish he wouldn't," my mother said, wiping her hands on a towel as she entered the room.

My father shrugged. "He owns a foot into the tree line. He can take whatever he wants from there. Promised me half the wood."

"I still wish he wouldn't. Don't see the point," my mother frowned.

My father shrugged again.

I silently agreed with my mother. Mr. Mason owned a big white house down the road and a few big fields to move his tractors around in. I didn't see how one more foot of space would make much difference. But I didn't say anything. I didn't play on that side of the woods anyway. The river was more interesting.

That afternoon, I watched as my father and Mr. Mason walked the property line, marking it with a rope in a straight line. Occasionally, they'd stop and argue over a tree that grew right on the line. If my father decided it was okay to cut, Mr. Mason would spray paint an "X" on it. There were a lot of "X's" before they were done.

After dinner, I packed a few things and headed over to Tilia's house. I stopped to say a brief hello to her mom and dad. They were younger than my parents, but really no different. They just seemed to like smooth lawns better than trees.

Sleepovers with Tilia always began in her little blue tent in the backyard. We'd roll out sleeping bags, turn flashlights on, read, and tell stories. And, after our parents were undoubtedly asleep in their beds, we would leave the tent for a midnight walk.

That evening, the stars were out in full force and the moon was waxing. Tilia and I approached the one-lane bridge that spanned the river. Our side of the river was filled with trees, but the other held more of Mr. Mason's fields, populated with rows of corn.

116

"I saw your daddy walking with Mr. Mason earlier," Tilia said at the middle of the bridge. The water moved dark beneath us and a chorus of frogs sang on the banks.

"Yeah, Mr. Mason's takin' down some trees on his side," I said.

"That's dumb. Why'd he wanna do that?"

I shrugged, feeling suddenly uncomfortable. I thought it was dumb, too, but my father seemed okay with it.

"Wish I had trees in my yard," Tilia continued. "If Mr. Mason tried to take them, I'd trample down his corn."

"They're his trees, just like the corn's his."

"Says who? I bet those trees were here first."

I shrugged again. We stood for a moment, listening to the frogs, watching the sky. Something to miss about the country is all the light. We could see everything we needed to see by the stars and the moon.

"Hey, wanna run through the corn?" Tilia asked, breaking the silence.

"Sure," I said, thinking only briefly before deciding that, yes, maybe Mr. Mason could afford to lose a little corn if he was taking our trees. And besides, it would be fun.

Tilia and I held hands as we crossed the bridge and jumped into the corn. We ran through the rows. We made zigzags and spirals, shrieking with laughter. Finally, breathless, we returned to the road, still holding hands. Feeling a little proud, we crossed back over the bridge and returned to the tent. Exhaustion overcame us and we fell asleep.

Walking back the next morning, I saw Mr. Mason already well underway with his cutting. His men's buzzing chainsaws made it look as though a knife had made a clean slice along the edge of the trees, leaving an unnatural wall.

When I made it back up to my house, I thought that it looked older somehow. Old as lines and boxes. But younger, too. Younger than the trees around it. Younger than the river and frog-song, and snail-shell spirals and the zigzagging of bees.

Dia de los Muertos
A. C. Crider

Audrey adjusted the handcuffs around her wrist as she watched the festival below. The day was turning slowly into dusk, and she listened to the mumbled voices and strumming of guitars.

"What are you thinking?" Red asked her.

"Just how lovely the evening is," Audrey replied.

She smelled the ocean. The ocean was salty, made her nose burn a little, but riding with it were smells of cinnamon, fresh-baked bread, alcohol, and a cookout. Downwind somewhere she could smell the rotting corpse of a beached humped back whale. There were no human smells there, making her feel sad for the forgotten body. Time moved too quickly sometimes.

"Are you disappointed?" Red asked. "So far they've tried to act macho. They've certainly smacked you around enough times."

Audrey shook her head.

"No. So far things are going perfectly." She leaned back against the wall, feeling the warm concrete and closed her eyes. Through the sounds of feet shuffling to Mariachi music and hands clapping, she heard a voice. It was a young man's voice, probably fifteen or sixteen years old. The register had not yet dropped into a low bass like a full-grown man's. He was in an alleyway close by, maybe two or three blocks away. She wished she knew more Spanish. The only words Audrey could pick up were *amor* (love) and *noche* (night).

"He sounds lovely, doesn't he?" Audrey said falling into a relaxation boarding on napping.

"He does. Must be hung up on a girl from school."

Audrey nodded and then the two of them laughed when they heard the boy's voice break on a high note. The laughter felt good. Ever since Audrey came back from her backpacking trip over the Appalachia a couple of years ago, things had been rough. Her mother and later her father both died in tragic animal attacks. Some sort of bear, maybe a wolf pack—the rangers said, but Audrey knew better. It had been her, and that weighed heavily.

"You still beating yourself up?" Red asked.

Audrey bit her lip. She stared out to the oceanfront, watching the waves break and the water turn darker as night approached.

"I miss them is all," she said. "Neither one of us knew about each other then. I know you wouldn't have hurt them any more than I would have. It's just . . ."

"What happened," Red finished.

Audrey nodded.

"That's why this trip is important," Red said. "That's why we came here, isn't it?"

Audrey straightened up. She picked at the spot where her kidnappers injected her. The drugs meant to make her drowsy left a bitter, salty taste in her mouth.

She looked at Red and smiled. "Yeah," she said. "That's why we came. To get away. After the backpackers, not to mention the rangers and that farmer and his livestock, we needed a getaway."

"Good," Red said. "I didn't want to think you still hated me."

"I never hated you," Audrey interjected. "I'm still getting used to you, that's all."

Red smiled and then there was silence. They listened as the mariachi started a new song. It was a love ballad Audrey could tell, even though she didn't know the words. It felt dreamy.

"Would you still have picked it had you known what would happen?" Red asked her after a while.

The stars were starting to come out over the ocean as night began to take over. The horizon was a mesh of oranges and vibrant pinks with a tinge of sea green. The moon had yet to show her face, but Audrey could feel its presence drawing near. Tiny, fluttery movements in her stomach started to flicker.

She thought of Red's question. It was a pretty violet flower. Bell-shaped and hanging in bunches. Mother moon stood over her watching as she plucked the velvet darlings from the ground, and, unbeknownst to her, was blessed that very night. It wasn't until she got home, sick and chilled with fever, that she began to worry. Yet she never did blame the flowers. Not even after scattering her father's ashes by the lake.

"I don't know," Audrey eventually said. "They were lovely, almost tempting. I'm not sure I could have said no to them even if I tried."

"Then what do you regret?" Red asked.

"Not getting to know you sooner. I . . . knew that something had changed. Waking up naked in the woods behind your house in full health when the last memory you had was coughing and being strung out with fever—something was different. And when it happened again, I almost didn't feel like me."

"I'm not a second personality," Red started. "I'm—"

Audrey took Red's hand into hers. It was much bigger than Audrey's but in no way less feminine. Her fingers were slender, like a piano player's yet strong. She looked into Red's green eyes and was reminded of how the two looked like twins. Same facial structure with differing colored eyes and hair. Red's was scarlet while Audrey's was blonde. But there was enough of her features in Red that Audrey couldn't deny the two were linked.

"I know," Audrey said. "You are a part of me as I am a part of you. Don't worry, Red," she said squeezing Red's hand, "I don't regret you."

Red sighed and smiled. Her stomach growled, too.

Night was approaching quickly now, they both could feel it. The bitterness of the drugs wore off. Audrey started to stretch, relaxing her back and legs. Her calves flexed then released, flexed again and let go once more like a sprinter ready for competition. There was a weight on her shoulders, a pulling back and forth. It was the sway of the water, she thought. The moon's pull had the same effect on her. She looked toward the night sky.

The sun was gone. No traces of warm light left. In its place was the moon, pregnant and bright, extra bright. Audrey felt a rush sweep through her. She still wasn't used to this part.

"Are you ready?" Red asked.

For the first time since the two came together, Audrey was ready. It never hurt, the transformation, not like the movies showed. It was more like drifting off to sleep, except Audrey never fully went under but just hovered somewhere between wakefulness and rest.

She could smell the fish in the ocean, could taste the tequila in the other room and could almost see the smoke from the burning cigarette one of her kidnappers smoked.

Audrey looked for Red but she was gone in the shadow. Only her glowing green eyes remained. She slipped off her dress feeling the warm night air prickle her skin. Her arms and legs grew longer. The handcuffs snapped like plastic, and Audrey felt herself getting bigger. Her finger and toenails grew, as did her canines. Suddenly she was in her natural state, with light brown fur. No, that wasn't totally true. Her other form, her day body, was just as much a part of her as this one was. She had to accept that. She and Red were one in every sense of the word now.

Audrey sniffed the air. Her stomach growled loudly, and then she found herself growling. The hunt was exciting this time. She and Red would work together, this time. Would feed, would chase, would live as one.

"This is where we start over," Red said.

"Yes, this is the way it should be," Audrey said.

And then came the howl.

Hereditary Traits
Cullen E McCurdy

—Head down!—Yeyek sent. Her telepathic voice hissed in a way her savaged chords couldn't manage right now—not that she wanted them to.

She extended one clawed hand to yank her charge back into the rooftop shadows. Vilv was swaddled in stolen civilian clothes where Yeyek still wore her black-trimmed-green dress uniform. Despite burned patches, tears at every hem and gaping holes where she'd torn its buttons loose, it shouted Admiral! Important! If they were caught, let the invaders think Yeyek was valuable. Vilv might yet escape.

Smoke and static discharge crackled the night air, and debris hurtled down to bury all horizons. It fell flaming, molten, red hot, ice cold, but always it fell. It would fall for hours, until the last of her ruined fleet buried itself upon the planet. Her flagship's hulk burned on the northern sky. Trailing debris and specks of loose fighters—scrambled too late—and slag like white-hot blood, it tumbled slowly in orbit towards the last light of the setting green sun. Its nemesis hung almost untouched in a sea of its kin, sharp-angled, long and tapering, a city-sized dark blot on the uncaring stars. It was surrounded by tiny swarming glints that might be strike-craft.

Or prison shuttles.

"Those aren't turncoats down there," she rasped aloud, throat singed from slagged-alloy fumes. She could still smell Deshfot's char-flesh; his agony-echoes rippled through her projection like light glinting from oblique metal. Was he still in there, helpless and in terrible pain, waiting for rescue that would never come? She hoped the Hatchmother had allowed him a quick death by decompression.

"Federation Regulars," she explained, sweeping a wary eye at the grim parade, "hardened bastards all." Young Vilv shuddered and drew her stolen poncho tighter; it didn't hide her tail's iridescent spine and plates, and the red-violet serum in the cracks between the golden plates reflected night fire in the worst way.

Yeyek used to envy females who shimmered like that. Now? Now it was just a glint for the enemy's eyes. Those horrible, too sharp eyes that saw you almost as easily standing still as running. After the eyes came the rifles, the hulking gleaming war-beasts that spat slugs wide as two of her fingers and thwipped horribly when they hit flesh. And they were so fast, fast for the kill as for nothing else, like there was some huge portion of the brains behind those black faceplates which woke only for bloodshed.

Vilv's red eyes shone cold with fear; Yeyek's ambers must look little better. The column thudded endlessly below as it had for the past half-hour, rank on rank of troops in transparent, color-shifting armor stamping even rubble flat.

All of them so tall, so coordinated. How did we ever believe we'd fight this? Yeyek thought. With the enemy's presence against her mind, she began to understand them. They were nervy, yes, and there was fear, but overwhelming all that was a feeling beyond emotion. It was an inexorable grind, forward momentum ponderous and inevitable and unchanging as time itself. This is what they do. It always has been. Yeyek closed in on herself before the feeling overtook her.

"Lieutenant!" one of the invaders called in their too-rapid speech, "This building cleared? Door's still on its hinges!"

"Neg, Captain!" another shouted back. "Sergeant Shurik, take four men, sweep it top to bottom. Anyone even twitches at you, drill 'em—remember, heart and spine if they give you the excuse! R&D wants the brains for study!"

Meit, now would be helpful! Yeyek hissed inwardly. In answer, a line of fire erupted from the building across the street, one the enemy had already cleared. Yeyek yanked Vilv up and pelted for the other end of the roof.

"Remember when I told you not to fly unless I said so? Well, I'm saying so!" she hissed.

"But your friend—"

"Meit knew what he was signing up for. We're not trying to win, we're trying to escape!" They leaped, holding themselves aloft over the ash-choked river below, over the toppled statues and cracked steel sculptures. The avenue behind erupted flickering yellow-white. Howling cracks and static charge slung tiny ripping things at the facade of Meit's building until it disappeared in cascading shards of metal and glass. Yeyek felt Meit's team die all at once, a dozen sharp cracks in her skull followed by chill, creeping tingles. Their minds might avert one slug, or a dozen, or a hundred, but sooner or later one got through. It only took one.

They landed on a balcony of stippled metal, reflecting the wan green moon's rise.

"We made it!" Vilv began. Yeyek nodded, turning for the doors ahead set with swirling patterns of black and copper.

Thwip.

Yeyek slapped a hand to her neck. Why her neck? There was nothing wrong with it. She heard something dripping—trickling?—and turned to Vilv. The girl fell against her, panicked hands on her throat. Something dark slicked out over the delicate golden fingers, so much of it from gurgling depths.

No, no, no! Yeyek hissed within. This isn't fair! She tore one of the sleeves from her uniform. Their snipers are supposed to target officers!

"Eyes on me, Vilv! Up here, Vilv! Stay calm, okay?! Stay calm!" Something thudded to the balcony beside her. Worked metal shrieked protests, then again, and again with two more thuds.

"Hey, scales! Hands in the air where I can see 'em!" Yeyek ignored the invader. Vilv's hands were on hers, clenching so tight and trembling so terribly.

"Can it, Phillips. Give them a moment."

Yeyek glared at the three figures looming above. These were different from the others; their bodies were all metal, shaped too regularly for nature. Only the eyes were the same, dark pupils on those bone-whites. Their faceplates were anchored to their foreheads. They were all six feet to her four, easily, but she didn't care. She forced their hateful speech into her mouth. "She's fifteen! Help her, damn you!"

"Alright, let me see," one said, kneeling beside her and prying Yeyek's hands open. "Keep her hands off, I need to see. Who is she?" The invader's heavy hand brushed something of polymer at her right hip.

Vilv shook her head, slapped feebly at Yeyek's hands. Her terror and resolve and fading will tugged Yeyek's mind, merest wisps hooked and tearing second by second.

—Let me die! Don't tell them, let me die!—the girl shrieked at her.

Yeyek looked at the glistening, pooling darkness. "She's the First Minister's daughter," Yeyek choked out.

The figured nodded, produced a single syringe, and stuck it in Vilv's neck-wound. Then came a pale yellowish patch and a second shot.

"Your cooperation is appreciated, Admiral Pozh," the figure said. Yeyek felt its presence push against her, a little nudge of the mind. Her last hope died. So, their minds can have gifts as well.

—She'll be allowed to live?—Yeyek sent, tentatively. Even the invader's telepathy, when it came, was inevitable.

—She may.—

Yeyek gulped and nodded, holding the figure's gaze. Green eyes. But for the round pupils and the white . . . whites, so like her own. Yeyek turned her attention on her body, felt for a rhythmic thudding and guided one claw to it. She tore a small hole in her uniform just above the beat.

—Here,—she sent.

The invader nodded sharply, plucked loose the pistol, and moved it towards Yeyek's mark.

Child's Play
An Excerpt from Sleepwalker: A Keyhole Novel
Sarah A. Kenney

9:23 a.m.

The noise of the coffee cup slamming on to the top of the café's marbled countertop startles me awake. The note in my hand falls onto the café's floor. I lean down at the same time as Cody to pick up the note, and we crash our heads together. I retort, rubbing my head while he continues to pick up the note.

"Did you stay up all night studying again, Ash?" He asks, rubbing his head while he sits on the stool next to mine, unfolding the crumpled note.

I reach to pull the note out of his hands, disturbed by the thought of anyone else reading it, but he has already read the words that are written in red.

"Down will go baby, cradle and all?" He raises a brow at me, *confused* at what a verse from the popular "Rock-a-Bye, Baby" would be doing written on a note that I had balled up in my hand.

"Felt nostalgic . . ." I joke, pulling the note out of his grip. I crumple the note back up and keep it squeezed inside of my fist.

"You have to let shit go, Ashley. It's just going to eat you up if you don't." He taps his finger against his coffee cup nervously.

I dismiss his lecture on how to "let things go" to become a better, freer living person, says the guy who can't decide what college he should attend, so he tries them *all*.

"So how did studying go?" He asks curiously, still tapping on the side of his coffee cup impatiently. I knew my silence was irritating him.

"Went fine," I say shortly, irritated by the repetitive.

He sighs, stiffening in his seat, his grip around the coffee cup tightens, "So . . . have you thought about it?" He asks hesitantly.

I know what he wants me to say but I don't feel it. I squeeze the note tighter in my palm. I can feel the panic inside of me . . . I couldn't go back to the way we used to be.

"I haven't really had the chance . . ." I avert the question like I'm dodging a bullet, which I am.

"Oh, come on, I've been waiting for an answer all year. I'm not just going to keep waiting, I think I deserve an answer." His voice cracks slightly, and he runs his hand through the loose strands of hair that hang above his right eye.

"Then it's a no, I don't have time for this. I don't have time for a relationship. Not after what happened." I stand up from the stool, leaving it pulled away from the bar. Another OCD thing that irritates him. I throw my styrofoam coffee cup and the note in the trash before leaving the corner café.

I walk out onto the curb, zipping up my jacket. The brisk cool air was a fair warning sign that winter would be here early in Chicago. Snow usually never fell in Chicago until the beginning of December, but everything about this year felt different than any others.

I hear the bell of the café door opening behind me. I can hear the quick zip of Cody's coat zipper behind me. I continue to press the crosswalk button in hopes it would stop traffic so I can avoid the mental breakdown he was about to have.

"I get you're going through a lot, Ash. If you think it didn't kill me inside what happened to her, then you are ridiculous. His voice is choked, "I can't imagine what you feel, but how long am I supposed to wait?" He asks, remorse and regret in his words.

"Stop waiting. I gave you an answer." I say emotionless.

The crosswalk finally lights up, signaling me to walk across the expressway.

"You say you don't have time but really, Ash, what else do you have?!" He yells from behind me.

On the other side of the street, I can breathe easier. I speed up my pace in case he is following me. I turn left on the sidewalk and head down Cassie Street to the little corner gift shop called "Flowers and Lace."

I had to pick up the flowers for her grave this week. I used to visit her every day, but the part of coping with what happened to her meant separating myself slowly from visiting.

Lacy, the short, spunky girl who owns the Flowers and Lace gift shop knows me by name. Three years I have gone into this same flower shop. She doesn't know who the flowers are for though. I never can get two words into discussing it without the lump forming in my throat. I feel like I am suffocating slowly every day, fading further away from the person I used to be . . . becoming an empty shell.

Cody wanted me to love him, how could I love him when I don't even love myself?

I grab the bundle of daisies, I was running out of types of flowers to lay on her grave, but I always imagined daisies would have been one of her favorites.

Lacy rings up the flowers and places them in a bag. I hand her the money for them, and she looks at me concernedly.

"How you feelin', hun?" She asks innocently, leaning on her elbow against the counter.

"I'm fine, just—" she cuts me off. "Tired." She finishes my sentence. I nod my head.

"You need to rest, you're too young to be so tired every day." She smiles faintly.

"Yeah," I reply. I have been tired every day for as long as I can remember.

I hear the bell to the flower shop open. It's Cody, again.

I sigh, too exhausted to care.

125

"What are you doing in here?" He asks me. Lacy pops her bubblegum behind the counter.

"Just getting flowers." I mutter to him, glancing back I tell her, "Bye, Lacy." before I walk past Cody and out of the gift shop.

"Are those for her grave, Ashley?" He asks, following me out of the gift shop. Irritation laces his words.

"You mean the grave you never visit? Yeah," I snip.

I walk down Hilsdale to "Child's Play Cemetery." I stop at the gates. My lungs feel tight whenever I visit, like I could never get enough air to feel normal again.

"I don't visit because she's not even there, Ash! You have to stop letting something that was an accident five years ago turn you into this person. It's like you're a prisoner of yourself . . ." He gestures to me like I don't see the person I have become.

"An accident?" I ask, taken aback by his words, whether he meant them or not. "That's exactly why I don't have time."

I walk over towards the small pink slab that has a little angel engraved into the stone along with the date, December 1, 2013. The flowers I left here last week, lilies, are dead. I replace the lilies with the daisies. The fresh scent of the flowers helps soothe the feeling of being surrounded by graves.

"I hope you like these ones . . ." I whisper, sitting down on my knees in front of her grave. I notice a small brown teddy bear propped up against the stone. I hadn't left it for her or seen it anywhere before.

I pick it up. Its fur is patchy and it only has one eye, the other is sewn into an "X.."." I smile faintly at the poor-looking bear and hold it in my lap when I cross my legs over themselves.

Cody stands back at the gate impatiently, not entering the graveyard. I can hear his coat crackle while he bounces to try to stay warm in the cool breeze.

"Hey, baby girl . . ." I whisper to her, placing the daisies in front of her grave.

"I can't wait till I get to see you . . ." I whisper to her with a smile.

The fresh scent of soil from the newest graves fill my senses. It makes me feel ill. No child should ever have to die so young. They never even get a chance to make mistakes like the rest of us.

It's so much harder to live than it would be to die, I tell myself. I know saying it to her grave wouldn't change anything. I couldn't save her, I couldn't go back and change what happened.

I hear his cough back at the gate. It breaks me away from the thought of how easy it would be to join her.

I shake my head. The sound of his irritation plays on a nerve like he is scraping his nails on a chalkboard. I place my hand on the gravestone.

"I'll be back tomorrow . . ." I promise.

It feels as though my heart is being ripped out of my chest when I turn away from her.

It never gets easier. Tomorrow always feels like I have to have hope that I'll wake up from this nightmare, with her in my arms. The past four years hasn't been the same. There was nothing left for me to hold on to in this city and Cody knew he wasn't ever going to be enough.

She wasn't here, but I had to tell myself—until I get to see her when I die, this is all I have left.

A grave.

In the White City
Brennan Quenneville

"Can you run?" he asked.

"I don't know," she said, prodding and testing her ankle. She stood up, took a few halting steps then winced and fell back to the ground.

"It's okay," he said. Eiko looked around the stone courtyard. Vines trailed over the heavy white slabs and grasses popped up out of cracks in the flooring, but nowhere did he see what he was looking for: a branch, a stick, something that might be used as a cane or crutch. "Come on," he said. He draped her arm over his shoulder and slowly stood, lifting her up with him. "Let's go."

The pair moved warily through the ancient and desiccated remains of the once great city of Ueto. They walked the King's Corridor, though they did not know to call it by that name. The King, and all his sons, had been dead for an age. The Kingdom, too, was gone, replaced at the time by warring nations that had long ago devolved into warring tribes. The City of Kings was a relic, a dead place inhabited by ghosts, forsaken by all living men as a place of fear and dread, an empty hallowed ground, a graveyard filled with uncounted and unnamed tombs. Eiko and Nisa, clinging to the boy's shoulder, drove on past vacant windows, abandoned sentry turrets, and decaying barricades. Long forgotten towers loomed up intermittently along the road, casting great shadows that reached out from the distant past to obscure the day's hot sun as it rose higher and higher. As thirst grew in the two young walkers, they were unaware that the great dike that ran to their left had once been a canal. It had carried water through all of the city in the days of the King's reign. Dust and wind were all that flowed through it now. It was a dark abyss amid the white stones of the city, a lurking fear for Eiko and Nisa. But Eiko held them on the road and the road followed the empty canal. It led somewhere. Out of the city, he hoped. There was no better alternative. They walked on.

At midday, Eiko stopped. He was drenched in sweat and breathing heavily. The sun had been beating on their faces all morning. "Let's sit for a moment," he said. He guided Nisa to a patch of shade beneath a stone awning overhung with tangled green vines. They shared sparing sips from Eiko's waterskin. In the light of the noon sun, the city gleamed white. Spots of green sprouted up wherever vines and lichen and grass had been able to take root.

"Thank you," she said. She looked into his face, but he continued to stare out at the white city. "Thank you for helping me. You didn't have to. I—I don't know why you did."

Eiko's eyes squinted at the brightness all around them. Almost imperceptibly he shook his head. "I helped you because help should be given where it is needed," he said. "Because we're not like them."

Nisa flexed her ankle and felt a twinge of pain run up through her leg and stab its way into her brain. "I can walk some of the way on my own," she said. "You'll wear yourself out carrying me."

"No," he said. "I won't. But we should get going. Come on." Again, he draped Nisa's arm over his shoulder and lifted her. She did her best to help him with the walking but her ankle was hurt, and he was, despite being thin and light himself, strong.

When the sun was sinking, its amber light tinting all of the stone city with a red hue, Eiko stopped them once more. This time they rested upon a dusty stone battlement, the remnants of a fountain that had run dry long, long ago. They climbed inside, its walls peering up over them, protecting them from the dead eyes of the dead city.

Eiko looked westward. Black shapes, like great and terrible birds, moved in the sky. He rubbed his eyes, and they were gone. He leaned back against the white stone rampart and was surprised to feel that it was cold against his skin. A cool breeze blew out of the east. For the first time that day Eiko was cold. He rubbed his arms with his hands to bring warmth into them, to get his blood moving again.

"How did we get here?" Nisa asked. "How did you get here? Do you remember any of it?" Her hands picked at corners of stone, where the heavy slabs had been fitted neatly together with a craftsmanship that had died years before. Her eyes stared past the stones to something more substantial but entirely out of reach.

"I don't," he said. "I don't remember. I don't know."

He put his arm around her and pulled her close. They stayed that way, huddled together for warmth, as the red sun sank over the white city and gave birth to a black night.

Soul

An Excerpt

Ranyas Senestela

The smell is the first thing that hits you, dense and putrid like a swamp on a hot summer day. The sounds hit you next but no one warns you about just how many there are. Sounds from bugs, flapping wings, inflating lungs, rustling grass, and the breath of something not visible rustling the leaves above me. These mortals though, skittering around on cobblestone roads with hand-pulled carts and muddied faces, were disgusting.

I'd never been to the mortal realm, their little lives reaching out to me from their souls, each pulsing and gold. It was odd, and the longer I stood in the shade of the trees alongside the small hovel of stone and thatch buildings, the more bewildered I became. These were the creations that countless family and friends killed over all those eons ago? It was maddening, watching them drudging through their lives, feeble creatures held together with nothing but meat and bone. How could such powerful souls be attached to such horrid and pathetic creatures?

Suddenly the rain had begun to fall and a flash in the sky brought me back to reality. As a Consort, it was my duty to come here and reap the souls that were set to detach from their mortal constraints. This had been the way of the world since the beginning; straining to regain immortality by collecting human souls was dirty business. The first human kill is said to be a divine experience, like elation during a battle or holding your child for the first time. Something from another realm and I had been hearing stories from my father for years about killing mortals.

"The sweetest thing you'll ever taste," I whispered to myself, glancing about as the mortals scurried into their shacks. The task is simple though; locate the red aura and detach the soul from the body. I crept out from under the trees now, rain running down my arms and face as I searched for the glowing red soul. It was simple to spot, nestled in a grove of trees at the base of a large rise. I didn't need to be patient, didn't need to savor this world of the weak and grotesque.

I approached the door, the mortal outside not even noticing me, like the flight of a bee toward her open window. I simply walked right into their tiny home, the glowing red aura pulsing brightly at me. There, laying on a bed of straw and pine needles was a senior woman. Her eyes were milky and blue, her skin leathery and her hair powdered white. She had turned toward me the moment I approached, her blank stare accompanied with a smile.

"I'm ready," I heard her whisper. "I've been ready . . ."

I didn't speak but instead plunged my dagger into her heart, a sensation overcoming me the instant she drew her last breath. It was electric, almost insatiable, gnawing away at every piece of me before bursting into thousands of rustling feathers. I had become stunned into silent ecstasy, feeling like I could collapse from all the energy but as quickly as it came, it left. I was abandoned, feeling want and need as I've never experienced before.

When I came to I saw that the woman on the bed had stopped breathing, her eyes lifeless as ever. I removed my dagger, noticing that there was no blood or mark on the mortal's flesh, just the vibrant blue stain still fresh on the blade. I heard the rustling of the younger woman outside the door and I turned, leaving the body where it was before exiting the hut. As I walked away, I could hear the loud wailing and sobs of the younger girl, a smile firmly plastered on my face. How weak and pathetic these mortals were. They could be picked off like flies, wingless and wriggling while being crushed into the dirt.

"I want more," I said, spotting my escort waiting for me in the tree line. His face was stern and his mouth set in a hard line.

"This isn't a sport," he said as I approached, the gateway opening before us. I wrinkled my nose at the writhing and swirling mist from the black abyss before me. This way of transportation was a crude imitation. "Come," he said, motioning for me to step through first.

"Ridiculous," I replied, my eyes narrowed.

"Master Dante," he replied, his eyes meeting mine. "We must get back. Your father will be waiting."

I couldn't help but growl at him, walking past him straight through the gateway, the swirling feeling of falling overtaking me instantly. That swirling black and misty air that stole my breath sucked me in and I spun, descending faster into the abyss. Moments later I felt my feet touch ground, taking a step forward and immediately feeling the light, almost sterile, air of the gateway lab.

"How did it go?" my father asked, watching me closely. We looked alike, as my mother often reminded me. Tall, stocky, light-haired, and deep gray eyes reflected my image but my father had a garish beard of gold that almost engulfed his neck.

"Well," I replied, placing my hand on the hilt of my dagger.

"Could have been better," Chester's voice whispered, his presence always close by. I smirked slightly and my father noticed, shooting me a sharp look.

"Chester wants more," I replied, feeling my dagger pulse below my fingers. "He's insatiable."

"Don't indulge yourself," my father shot back, turning from me now. "Come, we'll be late."

"I don't see why I must choose a bride," I groaned, falling in line behind him. "I'm still young and have decades, if not centuries, to decide."

131

"Don't be such a child," my father retorted, glancing back at me over his shoulder. "You're the heir of the Caligo family and it's time you accepted that."

"I don't see how an alliance will make a difference," I replied, making my father stop in the middle of the simple white hallway. "In the long run, it doesn't really matter how powerful we get or how many powerful family members we can boast. We'll still be doing the same thing our people have been doing for millennia."

"Consorts, Guardians . . . we're all the same just with different tasks," I continued, crossing my arms over my chest. "We should just crush them now, while they're weak and take over the council—"

I saw it coming but didn't expect the speed of my father's fist at it met my jaw with a crunch. I was sent sideways, knocking into the wall and falling to my knees. My jaw stung and ached and I could feel the blood pooling in my mouth, spitting defiantly on the floor before coming to my feet again.

"A soft spring boy like you can't possibly understand what is at stake here," he growled, glaring down at me through his beard. "I won't pander to your ignorance or your stupidity. You'll do as I say until you prove yourself worthy of my title."

"Mindless brute," Chester said, the anger pulsing from my hip. It had been torn from my control, anger welling in the pit of my stomach as I sprang toward my father. My dagger was firmly grasped in my hand and the hilt almost burned my palm as I swung, my father ducking almost instantly. He didn't even look confused or angry as he grabbed my collar and flung me into the whitewashed walls again.

I heard something crunch and I felt the stinging sensation spreading from my leg as I fell to the floor again. Every nerve in my body was set aflame now, my breath stolen away as my father looked down at me, writhing in pain. He'd never used his Sangveris on me before and the harder I struggled, the worse the pain became. What angered me more was that he wasn't the least bit amused at my pain, my hand reaching out to try and shakily grab his boot.

"You're pathetic," he replied, the pain ceasing as my entire body convulsed. "My own son, unable to even activate his Sangveris, trying to attack me in my own home."

"Go to hell!" I gasped, trying desperately to regain control of my limbs.

"Don't you see, boy?! We are in hell," he spat, grabbing me once again by my shirt. He hoisted me up and slammed me against the wall, our faces only inches apart. "It's finally time you understood that."

We both stood there, gazing at one another before my father let go of me. My legs felt like they would collapse under me, my hand reaching out to grab the wall. He didn't do this to amuse himself or make a point. He didn't even care to see me as a challenge; simply a pawn to do his bidding and this was his weakness. He always severely underestimated me and in that moment, I'd have gladly plunged my dagger into his heart. He only stared down at me now, the same stern and detached expression he always had on his face.

"We're going to meet your mother and her guests in the library," he said to me, his voice calm and cool as if nothing had even happened. I could feel the anger welling in my stomach again but I had to stop. I couldn't challenge him again; not so soon.

"Yes father," I replied, straightening myself as I bent to pick Chester up off the ground. My father only growled, turning to lead me back down the hall toward what was presumably my bride to be.

"*Soon my friend,*" Chester cooed, a slight smirk spreading over my lips. "*The oaf has no idea, even now . . .*" I kept pace with my father as he strode down the hall, knowing full well that this wouldn't be the first time he'd make the mistake of striking me.

Tabby Gingerbottom: Private Eye!
Sarah Sorensen

My name is Gingerbottom. I'm a British shorthair, and I solve crimes. It's that simple. So when somebody filched the flask of brandy out of Mr. Tuttle's top desk drawer, he sent immediately for me: Tabby Gingerbottom, Private Eye! At my arrival, the old man bid me to come into his office and examine the scratches around the keyhole of his desk drawer. With my cobby body style and prodigious tummy flaps, it took extra exertion to hop up onto the desk chair. I tried not to scratch the leather upholstery, but it was useless. I had left a mark, a pinhole at most. Tuttle cleared his throat in annoyance.

"The scratches look like somebody took a screwdriver to the lock," I said. "How old is that son of yours now?"

I'd seen this kind of handiwork before.

"Walter, why he is only just turned fourteen!"

Tuttle called for the boy and as Walter sulked into the room, I sunk down into the seat of the chair and Tuttle turned me toward the wall so as to conceal myself. Walter was the type of youth whose newfound height was not matched with much strength, and consequently he always looked like he was slightly bent forward—gangly like a new branch on a houseplant, bending under its own weight. I eyed Walter, trying not to let my hindquarters rise as I felt my chin sinking ever closer to the chair seat. After all, I had been watching him from the mirror effect in the large windows of Tuttle's office. When the boy had entered, it had startled the old man and the old man had instinctively turned me toward the windows. Now Walter began sneezing profusely.

"Sorry, Gingerbottom. The boy has allergies," Tuttle said. Then, turning to the boy, "Gingerbottom seems to think that you might have taken my brandy flask. What have you to say for yourself, Walter?"

"What are you talking about?"

The boy was insolent, perhaps drunk even now. The redness in his eyes was visible, even in his ghostly doppelganger which I was scrutinizing in the window.

Tuttle turned the desk chair slowly to reveal: Tabby Gingerbottom, Private Eye! Walter's red watery eyes stared at me in disbelief. I had once foiled a younger Walter in his vain attempts to steal extra cookies, crayon his name onto the bathroom walls, and once I had put an end to his sinister effort to conceal a canine in the sweat sock abyss that is his closet. I purred, tossing a nail husk from my front paw. It fell at Walter's feet and he sneezed again.

"That's right, I'm back," I said.

"Look, Gingerbottom. I don't have time for this. I have soccer practice tonight and I can't deal with these allergies right now."

"Oh, I think you can, Walter," I whispered, shaking my loose fur vigorously in his direction. "I think you will be quite cooperative."

The melodramatic boy was nearly gasping now, professing that he could hardly breathe. Sure, he was red-faced, but what lush isn't?

"Walter," Tuttle said, "If *you* drank the brandy, please just tell Gingerbottom and we can get on with your punishment. Gingerbottom is a much sought after Private Eye, and frankly we cannot afford him, what with your mother's bestsellers being remaindered and my antique pipe collection rapidly dwindling in sales on eBay."

But the boy was obstinate. He grumbled and sneezed and claimed abuse, meandering off to the kitchen for a snack—no doubt believing that the chocolate chip cookies from his dear old mother would cover his foul, alcohol-soaked breath.

"Looks like we are doing this the hard way," I said.

I unsnapped the pouch I keep about my neck and procured my magnifying glass, a piece that I had fashioned especially for me. The magnifying glass company added a customized cardboard handle for my ease of use. Clasping it now, I took a better look at the scratches. The inspection proved as useful as it was frustrating—the scratches were perhaps Tuttle's own drunken scratches made as he vainly sought the keyhole. My large eyes and narrow pupils betrayed me.

"That's right, Gingerbottom. The scratches are made of my own shame. Yet, this I promise you, the flask was removed by some no-good-nick and its safe return is worth even your hefty sum.

"You see, Gingerbottom, the flask was something of a family heirloom. Great-Great-Great Grandma Mitzi bought it off an orphaned dwarf during a midnight carnival of freaks. Mitzi was a rebellious young woman, off to experience the world on her own. When she happened upon this carnival of dark pleasures, she was already somewhat refreshed by a nip of her father's gin. Thus, she took the dwarf's flask of moonshine and wandered off with it. Due to her no doubt increased . . . sociability . . . she ummm, she became immodest with the half-man, half-lady, and it was this . . . err . . . experience that propagated our noble bloodline. Mitzi gave birth to twins that winter, a boy and a girl, of course.

"Since that time, our family has assumed that the flask has magical powers, offering increased fertility. That is partially why I keep it locked up—but now, if Walter . . . God save us!"

Tuttle broke into tears as he imagined the awkward houseplant boy copulating with some ragamuffin neighbor, populating his home with a litter of sulky pups, pink skinned and fleshy. I cannot say that it did not make my own fur bristle, and I attempted to pat Tuttle on the back of his thigh. However, the stretch from the height of the chair seat to his thigh was simply too great, and I am embarrassed to admit that I became entangled, resulting in a panicked swipe at his thigh and my instinctual pull back. After clipping him, Tuttle shot bolt upright and let forth a high-pitched holler, increasing my panic. There may have been some incidental tearing of his fabric. I did not have the heart to mention the snag. Let him assume he caught it on some jagged corner someplace.

I put the magnifier in my teeth and moved toward the staircase. Walter sneezed as I whisked by, a fine mist of my blown coat wafting in the air. After ascending the stairs, I hooked a sharp right into Walter's room. This was familiar ground, indeed. The tang of his acrid smelling clothing often sent me hopping back, only to be forced to re-approach and paw at the pit-stained unpleasantness. Walter. That boy had been nothing but trouble all of his life.

Using my magnifying glass, I sifted through his notes. "Biology test 9-15." "Spanish quiz 10-18." These notes were months out of date. The boy's record-keeping skills were perhaps tainted by some demon liquor coursing through his blood. Then, I found it. Well, not "it" exactly, because "it" would probably mean the flask. What I found was a magazine of questionable nature, a "swimsuit issue." The model on the cover was some photo-shopped filly with long legs and a big blond mane and a tan—a sort of human palomino. The boy's perverse pleasures were becoming disturbingly apparent. Terrified by what I had seen, I drove under the bed for a bit of solace, but alas! As I drove under the boy's bed, I found an underpants jungle. Lodged within a pair of tightie-whities, I saw a silvery light. I leaped back, aghast. Then, forcing myself not to vomit, I walked back up and slapped aside the yellowed fabric. There lay the scrolling patterned flask.

"Well, Tuttle," I sighed, "It looks like you are going to be a grandfather."

And with that, I began batting the flask down the hall. My work was done.

Please stay tuned for the next adventure of Tabby Gingerbottom: Private Eye! Gingerbottom will be forced to confront the mystery of the old bank slip. . .

Under the Surface
Moya Tobey

My fingers tremble in the sub-zero winter air. I didn't bother to don the proper winter gear before coming to the ice-covered pond. It seems wrong to be warm and comfortable at James' grave. The snow-covered ice crunches beneath my feet, and I carefully shuffle over the frozen pond. My knees quiver and every step makes the journey a million times harder. The further I move away from land, and the closer I get to the center of this death trap, the more violent my trembling becomes. Something warm slides down my cheeks. It's been a year, and I still can't gather enough strength to get to the exact same spot where it happened.

A jolt explodes through my body when my knees hit the ice. A sob escapes my throat, passing my dry and cracked lips.

"I'm so sorry, James," I cry. "It was all my fault. I shouldn't have let you get so far ahead."

My shoulders quake, lips and chin quiver. Head hung low, I weep. If it wasn't for me, James would still be alive. If I had simply skated a little faster, my brother wouldn't have drowned. The ice shocks my hand with its temperature.

Crack!

I let my eyes wander over my surroundings. A fog covers my train of thought; everything is clear but not in focus. It seems like there is a large crack in the ice a foot away from me, but that can't be. The pond should be covered in 6 inches of ice by now. I let my gaze fall back to the ice. It's so cold and harsh. Suddenly something appears beneath the ice, and I scream. The ice is mocking my pain. Showing me the face of my brother. My grief must be so strong that I'm starting to hallucinate. I rub my eyes and peer back at where I saw James' face. The pale, lifeless stare of my brother still stabs my already shattered heart.

Curiosity overtakes me, and I crouch down toward the ice for who knows what reason. Then I'm screaming again. James' corpse is no longer lifeless but laughing at my horror.

Crack!

The fissure in the ice gets bigger. So, I wasn't imagining it. The line of impending doom races toward me, but I am frozen. Perhaps it is my subconscious reminding me of what I had done, telling me this is how I deserve to die. With an air of finality, the ice splits apart and I feel a surprisingly warm hand pull me under.

I know it's my brother dragging me to my death—or his ghost. I don't even try to escape—this is what I deserve. The light above slowly fades away, and I wait for the darkness to take me. My lungs burn until I can't stand it any longer. I breathe in a mouthful of water, waiting to drown. But nothing happens. In fact, I'm breathing. Underwater. How is this possible? I shift my gaze to my brother's form who is still dragging me deeper under the surface. How is any of this possible? It isn't. I have to be dreaming. That's the only possible explanation. And since this is a dream, I mind as well enjoy this time with my brother. Even if it isn't real.

James looks exactly as he did before he drowned. Shaggy blond hair, gleaming green eyes. Such a young and innocent face. A face that wouldn't see the light of day again.

In front of me—or below, I'm not sure—a bright light grows in the distance. As we come closer, it takes the shape of a kingdom. James abruptly stops, and I float to his side. He remains silent for a moment, staring at the kingdom. I have so much to say but sense that the quiet is necessary.

"I'm not mad at you." James breaks the silence.

"But you drowned because of me. I'm sorry." I blurt.

James turns his face toward me and gives me a queer look.

"Why are you apologizing?"

"It's my fault that you're dead," I whisper.

At that exact moment, I can see that James is so much wiser than me. He may still look like a child, but his facial expression is that of a man who has lived a thousand lives.

"This is my home," he gestures toward the kingdom. "My mortal body may be gone, but I am very much alive. Actually, I came to save *you*."

"Me?" I ask.

"Yes. You have the opportunity to live here when you die, like me, but there is something you must do. You have to let go."

I snort, "Let go? How is that going to change any of what happened?"

"It won't but," James pauses. "You feel responsible for my death. The guilt of not being able to save me drags you down every single day."

"Please stop."

"If you want to be rid of that guilt, and live a forgiven life, then you must let go." James insists.

"It can't be that simple," I mumble and close my eyes.

"But it is! Just *let go*, Alethea."

I open my eyes, and my room greets me. It was just a dream. Even so, I can't shake what he said. James is right. Guilt dogs me every day, some days I can't even stand to look at myself in the mirror. This may be my only hope. I so desperately want to live in a way that would make my brother proud. This just might be the way. I glance around the room and sit up in bed. No one is around.

Just let go, Alethea.

I close my eyes, take a deep breath, and let go.

Etched in Steel
Andrew Ronzino

Nustorue's injured wing made it difficult to fly, but he refused to rest. He wasn't sure if the Raiders were still chasing him and he didn't want to risk stopping. Sweat poured from him as he raced through the rainforest, weaving around trees and vines. He wouldn't let his wound slow him down, not now. Not when he was the last of the spies left alive.

When he reached the dense patch of trees that hid the secret back entrance to the city he landed and put his palm on one of the trunks. The moss covering the tree read his handprint and the large stone at the base moved aside. He dropped into the hole, using his wings to slow his descent. He touched down and folded his wings on his back, wincing from the pain, and ran the rest of the way through the vast underground.

The council room doors were shut which meant there was a meeting in session. No interruptions were allowed unless it was an emergency. This qualified. Two Vala guards holding pikes kept watch outside the doors. Nustorue knew them from his late-night resistant meetings, acquaintances more than friends.

"They're in session, Commander," one of the guards said, holding up his hand.

Nustorue caught his breath and ignored the stitch in his side. "I know, Salasos. This is urgent. The Raiders are coming."

Salasos shared a glance with the other guard, Teelana. She nodded. Salasos nodded back and opened the door. Nustorue thanked them and jogged in.

Inside the ornate council chamber, the decor was mostly ceremonial. Four polished steel pillars supported the stone ceiling. The whole room portrayed an opulence that no longer existed anywhere else in the country. Nustorue approached the curved wooden desk where the five Vala regents sat arguing. They stopped and stared at him.

"Commander," a senior Vala named Erina said. "We feared you and your team was dead." The feathers on her wings, once brilliant white, were graying; her silver hair was braided. Her stern eyes were fading from their bright luminescent green.

"I am the only one who survived, Ma'am, everyone else is dead," he said. "I have come to report on our mission to determine the state of affairs with the Raiders."

"Please tell us what you've learned," a soft-spoken regent named Liou said.

Nustorue cleared his throat. "While we were scouting, we were discovered. I was the only one to escape. I tried to hide, but they found me and chased me for hundreds of miles. But, before we were found, we learned the Raider Nation is planning a full out attack of Lestara. They have pinpointed our military's weakest defenses along the border and here in the city. They are going to invade within hours. They may already be marching. Raider strike teams were gathering along the mountains and preparing to move into our land when I fled."

Silence filled the council room. The five regents shared glances with each other. Finally, Regent Erina sighed. "We know."

"I don't understand, Regent," Nustorue said, confused.

"We have known of this invasion for weeks. The Raiders have been threatening us for the better part of a year now."

Nustorue held back rage. Twelve people on his team died to gather that information and the regents already knew? He gritted his teeth and spoke through them. "Forgive me, I still don't understand. Why did you send in spies if you already knew?"

"To assess the strength of the Raiders," Erina said. "When you didn't return two days ago like you were supposed to, we assumed you were all dead, which, given the skill of your team, told us all that we needed to know."

"I was the only one left alive. I was trying to get home, but it was difficult. Why wasn't I told what the mission really was? We were told the objective was to get intel about the border and the strange Raider sightings in that area. If I had known—"

"We needed to test the strength of the Raiders," Regent Costra said. He was so old his eyes and hair were completely gray. "Your team provided that opportunity."

Nustorue bit his lip and clenched his fists to keep himself from lashing out. His team was used as a test, his people's lives meant nothing to the regents. He swallowed the knot of anger in his throat. "With all due respect, Regent Costra, if you needed to know the strength of the Raiders, I could have prepared my team for such a mission, and twelve good men and women would still be alive."

"Watch your tone, Commander," Costra said.

There was silence for a moment. Nustorue offered no apology.

"The loss of your team is regrettable and sad," Erina eventually said with no hint of sympathy in her voice. "Their sacrifice shall not be forgotten, and their families will be informed of their heroism. We are preparing to deal with the Raiders."

"Good. Shall I start building a new team?"

"No. We will not be fighting the Raiders," Costra said.

"What do you mean?"

"We cannot fight them, they are too strong," Costra said, frowning. "The Raiders have already conquered Cor'el and Elventra. Lestara will fall like they did if we fight."

"But you said—"

"What I meant was we are making a deal with them," Costra said. "When your team didn't return, we knew how strong the Raiders had become on our border. We've drafted a letter of surrender and signed it. We will be accepting Raider occupation."

Nustorue stood stunned. He couldn't believe what he heard. He opened his mouth to argue.

"Our decision is final," Costra said. "Thank you for reporting in. You are a fine soldier, Commander Nustorue. You're dismissed."

Dejected, Nustorue bit his tongue, gritted his teeth, and bowed respectfully to the regents. He turned on his heel and walked past the two closest steel pillars. The history of the four known eras of the Vala people was etched into the four steel pillars. Each one spoke of a past grander than the declining nation they had become over the last three hundred years. He stopped and skimmed some of the histories on the left column.

"Is there something else, Commander?" Liou said.

Turning to the leaders of the Vala, he did his best to keep his anger in check. "They're going to enslave us, you know. The Raiders aren't known for being kind to the people they conquer. Occupation means we're in for hard times. People will lose their freedom or lives at the slightest resistance."

Liou nodded. "Occupation is better than all of us being slaughtered."

Nustorue shook his head. "Many will be slaughtered anyway."

"We are surrendering to save lives," Costa said.

"I believe you, but it doesn't mean it's right. None of the previous Lestara regents would've surrendered without fighting first." He walked out.

The doors closed and Nustorue stood there trying to avoid the panic he felt rising inside him. Pain spiked in his wing.

"What's going on Nustorue?" Salasos said. "You look pale."

Nustorue stood up straight and tall. He puffed out his chest. "The resistance begins now."

"Impossible," Teelana said. "We're not ready."

"We have no choice," Nustorue said. "The Raiders are coming and the regents are choosing to surrender without contest. We must act now, but our target will now be the Raiders. Spread the word. Lestara will etch our story in steel."

Some Days
Breezy White

There were some days that we looked at with such fervent. The air was warm, our bodies raw and, back then, we didn't truly understand how good it was to be alive. But we could taste it. There wasn't a day where we left the lake, even though the holes at the bottom tried to eat us whole, and there wasn't a night that we didn't stop to think "maybe sneaking out of our tents right now isn't the smartest idea—we could get eaten by Dog Man," but we charged full-fledged. If anyone caught us in their peripheral vision, while we spoke of myths that shook me and kept me younger than my age, we would try and grab hold of our fear and *drown* it and crush it and make it disappear because we never wanted to be bigger or braver than we did back then.

Guess Who Would You Do?
Justin Gawel

"Does your person have a beard?"

"No," I replied. I shot a little head jab over at Terry. "Your person," I paused as one of my eyebrows popped up. "Would you do them?"

Our aging house was dead-silent and my words seemed to linger in the air as Terry could only sit there, dazed.

I repeated my question. "Come on, Terry. Yes or no?" This was supposed to be a quick game. We had dinner plans after all.

"It's just a picture, though."

"Sure. A picture, like in a magazine, or on TV, or in a fantasy . . ."

"But it's just, just a head?"

"Yes," my eyes narrowed, "with a mouth, Terry." Imagination needn't be this painstaking. "Probably some feet." I continued, "Soft hands. A butt, perhaps."

"I suppose . . ." Terry perused the card, wistful. The hesitation persisted and I quietly flipped down all of the faces on my game board of characters I knew Terry would have unquestionably sexed.

Our reservation was for seven sharp. Tonight was an overdue extravagance for us and it would be nice—even if only for a few hours—to pretend we belonged in society's upper crust. I assured myself that this time I would not ask if the kitchen served any meatloaf or if the jazz quartet knew any Meatloaf. This evening's dalliance with privilege would be decadent, delicious, and not again end in public disgrace.

The card remained there, front and center, as Terry continued scrutinizing. "Am I drunk in this scenario?" I thought my initial question had been exceedingly binary; I hadn't expected any follow-ups, but I said *sure, if you want.* I qualified, though, that this meant tipsy and a little mean—like maybe mix up someone's new baby's name with their dog's name. Sassy drunk and not at all vindictive and trolling for any amount available friction.

I flipped down all of the remaining attractive faces: possibilities where Terry wouldn't have had to self-handicap a decision by being under the influence. Skipping lunch today was catching up with me now. The pain would be worth it. However, I would absolutely not be able to stomach "Unfortunately we gave away your table, but you two could see if they could squeeze you in at Burger King."

"When do I meet this person?"

"Come on, Terry." Two follow-up questions? There was no hiding it now. "Do you think you meet them, like, during The Reformation or on the Oregon Trail?" I tried to calm myself as Terry sat, just this meek, puzzling lump across the table. "No, Terry, you meet them on any normal day like today." I stopped, "Except in this hypothetical you can take your time because you don't have goddamn dinner plans!" I snapped down four faces on my game board, all varying iterations of nothing-to-write-home-about where the time period would not have mattered. Real "rest-stop-in-Ohio" types.

Only two faces remained now on my game board: both aesthetic monsters with one foot still in puberty and the other in the grave. If we missed this reservation—I don't know—I'd need to start taking a different route to work. The restaurant would be no more than another beacon of failure, like the truck driving school, the upscale bistro where we'd been ridiculed, and The Gap where I'd pushed that kid.

The sun had set and the house was growing dark. Terry starred the card down, head shaking slowly. "I don't know," Terry said as I stood up and flipped on a lamp, "even if I was a little drunk, or randy, and there was a blindfold." We were going to have to whip through all five lights to make it by seven now. "So as long as they didn't have some sort of love-potion pheromone or a weapon, I would have to say no."

"Jesus Christ, Terry," I recoiled with a grimace and a sigh, supposing that's where we'd draw the line on imagination.

Sitting back up and surveying a board with three-quarters of the faces remaining, Terry refocused. "Does your person have a hat?"

"No." I flipped down one of my remaining options, who seemed dramatically less likely to own a weapon or elicit erotic help from chemical warfare. "Your person is Alex."

"Dammit, yeah."

"Great. Now go get your dumb shoes on."

Unhinged
Amanda Lott

The sturdy metal chairs in the interrogation room were designed to be uncomfortable. They were, in Lovett's opinion, a method of legal torture, the purpose of which was simply to break even the strongest of wills, mainly after being forced to sit in them for a prescribed period of time. After sitting in that harsh metal chair for close to an hour, a thought occurred to Lovett, that perhaps this wasn't the most effective way of coaxing information out of their captives. After all, most were allowed to stand and stretch their legs, pace the floor until some seasoned detective who reeked of stale cigarette smoke and cheap coffee came in the room and ordered them to sit down and start singing like a canary. But Lovett was not afforded this particular luxury. His body was rigid, but not in a forced way, his wrists bound by metal handcuffs which were connected to the same cuffs around his ankles by a thin but heavy chain. He gave the chain a shake, as if he were testing its strength, but barely moved from where he sat.

Lovett closed his eyes and took a deep breath. He opened his eyes slowly and let them dart across the room, making a note of each and every single detail about the room around him. The industrial clock on the wall, its face hidden behind a metal grate, ticking out of sync with Lovett's heartbeat. But Lovett breathed slowly, carefully, allowing his heartbeat to finally line up with the rhythmic ticking of the clock. The table in front of him had a metal top, though it was warped in places where a cup or something had been left to sweat for too long. The silence was broken only when the heavy metal door screeched open, its hinges crying out for some kind of lubrication or maintenance. The sound was unreasonably loud and filled the room in an instant and pierced the silence like nails dragging across a chalkboard. But Lovett remained still. Trained.

Waiting.

Two heartbeats later, Special Agent Elijah Carey pushed the heavy metal door closed behind him, allowing the door one final screech before the latch clicked into place. Agent Carey looked ragged, days of sleeplessness appearing as dark circles under his eyes, matching the days of scruff growing in patches on his jaw. He took a deep breath and advanced slowly on the table, the heels of his dress shoes clicking on the tiled floor. Agent Carey's focus remained as steely as he could handle, focus set on the man sitting stationary at the table now between them. In one hand, the manila folder which contained the file that Agent Carey often referred to as Lovett's greatest hits.

"Accomplishments," Lovett, in a moment of brazen pride, gently corrected.

Lovett's eyes shifted from a single stained spot on the wall to the folder in Agent Carey's hand, and he felt the slightest smirk tug at the corner of his mouth. Agent Carey watched Lovett's reaction, again studying him as if he were looking for some kind of crack in Lovett's granite exterior. Taking a breath, Agent Carey dropped the manila folder onto the table and leaned in, shifting to look Lovett straight in the eye, again trying to break his laser focus. But Agent Carey had yet to shift Lovett's attention, even an eyelash.

Agent Carey cleared his throat. "So, what happened?" he asked, his voice joining the ticking clock as the only sound in the room. Both were soon accompanied by the buzzing of the fluorescent light overhead. By speaking Agent Carey was, yet again, trying to catch the younger man off guard in any way, hoping to gain some sort of upper hand in this situation.

But Lovett remained steadfast, the hint of a smile vanishing completely from his face. The resolve that Agent Carey felt may have been breaking returned in full force. Lovett folded his hands on the table in front of them, the chain between the handcuffs rattling in the process. Lovett's silence persisted, even when Agent Carey's words demanded some kind of answer from him.

"You aren't going to tell me, are you," Agent Carey inquired, and again he was greeted by silence. Lovett continued to sit perfectly still behind the table, his fingers now splayed across the surface, furthering his connection to his surroundings, to the entire building around him. Agent Carey, again thinking for the briefest of moments that he'd started to gain some kind of upper hand, let out a little snicker and took a seat at the table across from Lovett, his own chair scraping against the hard tile floor. "You slipped up, that's all. You did, though. You slipped up and that's why you're sitting here in this dank, shitty room with me right now."

Lovett's gaze was still focused on the wall behind Agent Carey, seeing right through him as if he were made of glass. It was only when Agent Carey spoke that Lovett's attention was finally pulled away from the wall. "Did I?" he questioned, almost comical in his mind. Agent Carey nudged the manila folder forward, slipping it up under Lovett's fingertips. Lovett didn't have to open the folder to know its contents. Again, Lovett smirked, and without lifting the cover he pushed the folder back toward Agent Carey. "Do you think I made a mistake? Or do you think my being caught was just part of the plan?"

"Part of the plan?" Agent Carey chuffed and sat back in his own uncomfortable metal chair, its feet again scraping against the floor from the force of his reaction. "Part of your master plan was to get arrested? That doesn't seem like a very smart move, Lovett."

At the assumption that Lovett was not, in every way, an extremely intelligent man, he sat up with his shoulders pushed back and shook the curls as well as the smile back from his face. "Plans can be convoluted, Elijah. You of all people should know that wisdom and knowledge aren't always as straightforward as you would hope." Each of Lovett's movements was slow, concocted. He brought his palms up from the cold metal table and folded them together in front of him, fingers intertwined as if he were praying. He looked up from his hands to Agent Carey and couldn't help but smirk again. "Regardless of its straightforwardness, or complete lack thereof in some cases, wisdom always has a way of drawing out the truth."

Agent Carey watched Lovett's every move; watched his fingers clench and unclench almost in time with his own heartbeat. Could Lovett even hear his heart beating behind his ribs? Agent Carey wondered this, wondered if Love could actually feel the hot blood coursing through his veins. His eyes turned to Lovett's, and for a split second, Agent Carey could see right down to Lovett's soul.

Or the dark expanse where Lovett's soul once was.

"Wisdom." Agent Carey drew in a breath and felt himself smirking at Lovett, an involuntary reaction to him. Lovett looked so young, though Agent Carey knew that Lovett's youth was not to be underestimated by any sense of the word. Other law enforcement officers saw how young Lovett was and were genuinely unable to believe that he was capable of the unspeakable horror that was painted all over the files that crowded Agent Carey's desk. "Wisdom. That's your specialty, right?"

For years, the focal point of Elijah Carey's work, of his entire career, were the lives of two people: Josh Lovett, the young apprentice who quickly surpassed his master, bent on showing the world that he was more than capable, and Tommy Moeller, the man, the master whose crimes were unparalleled in the history of the bureau's serial division. How these two found one another was not a complete mystery, but Agent Carey had yet the opportunity to determine all of the nuances of their story.

How did one source of evil find another? The story needed both protagonists to be complete. And Agent Carey always had one or the other, but never both. Agent Carey had bits and pieces, a clue here and a hint there, but didn't have all of the details. Didn't have the full puzzle. And that's what he wanted; he wanted the full story, he wanted to know the story from start to finish.

"All the riddles," Agent Carey proceeded. "All of the clues that were found and deciphered. It was all planned. They were all left out in the open for us, right? Like breadcrumbs?"

Lovett chuckled, a slight sneer pulling at the corners of his mouth. "Breadcrumbs are left behind by a larger animal, usually. To make sure that the smaller animals eat," he replied in a calm and flat voice from behind the smirk. "Only the larger animal can truly know their purpose. The smaller animals are just grateful to have them. Otherwise, they would starve right where they stood."

Agent Carey narrowed his eyes, staring Lovett down as he had many times before, looking for any type of small cracks or fissures in the rough, solid exterior. But Lovett truly was like a slab of polished marble; nothing Agent Carey could do or say would break him.

"So what you're saying is that we're the smaller animals, and that you're killing us to keep us alive?"

Lovett's attention immediately shifted to Agent Carey and raised a slight eyebrow. "A distinct possibility," he replied quickly. "It's also a possibility that you feel alive simply because I've killed again. I honestly never imagined a scenario where you got more out of it than I did, yet here we are. Born into a brand-new world."

Agent Carey became visibly frustrated and stood from the table. He scooped up the manila folder and tapped his chest with its rounded edge. He turned and made his way toward the exit, and with one hand on the knob he paused. "There's just . . . one thing that I'm curious about." Agent Carey turned back to see Lovett still sitting, remaining just as steady as he had throughout their short conversation. "If I ask you a question, will you be able to answer it without another question?"

Lovett tittered silently. "I . . . supposed that depends on the question," he responded, the calm in his voice shaking just a bit.

Agent Carey smirked, wondering if he finally gained a little ground. Wondering if Josh Lovett was finally starting to crack, if he was finally ready to break. Agent Carey cleared his throat. "Where's Tommy?" he questioned. "Right now. Do you know where Tommy is?"

Her Majesty
Melanie Noell Bernard

I hummed to myself as I brushed my hair, watching it gleam in the mirror. I counted every stroke. Because it had to be precise. I had to run the brush through exactly 106 times, otherwise it would all be ruined. And I couldn't risk ruining my hair.

Just as I placed the brush down on the table—having reached one-hundred and six—a knock sounded on the door.

"Right on time." I smiled to myself in the silver surface, drawing on the face that didn't frighten the humans, the one I was told to wear. "Come in!"

The latch clicked. The door swung open with just the faintest creak at the end to signal it was completely ajar. The gentle thud-thud of footsteps followed as he crossed the room.

"How are we this morning?"

Through the mirror, I saw him. The new one. His hair was swept to one side, sleeked with enough gel to make it shine. His ivory coat was pressed and hung down to his knees as stiff as though it had been over-starched. But none of that mattered.

My smile dropped. My eyes met his in the mirror and all color drained from his face as he started to quiver.

"Y—Your Majesty," he added in a blabber of syllables. He dipped his head as his fists clenched, causing the strange item in his left hand—the one called a 'clipboard'—to rattle.

Rage burned through me at his insolence, at his ardor. He had been told. He had been instructed and *still* he managed to screw the whole thing up! How *dare* he ruin my perfect morning!

"A thousand and three dozen apologies, Your Majesty." His voice regained some of its strength and he bent his knees to lower himself below my own head but dare never bend at the waist lest creases find his jacket or let his hair fall out of place.

Though he had spoken improperly, he knew the appropriate way to apologize and I could not find it in my heart to punish him . . . today. "Very well, thank you." I donned the smile once more.

Rising, he drew the clipboard up and glanced down at it. All his earlier quivering vanished as he made perfect eye contact with me.

But that second's hesitation lashed me across the cheek. My teeth ground together inside my wide smile, baring my anger. How dare he show his face while still learning! Had no one told him? Surely they must have! It was his second day already and yet he still had to look?! What was this? Some play rehearsal?!

"On today's agenda . . . ." While his eyes met mine, it was clear he was not truly meeting my gaze. His eyes had glazed over. It was the look I had seen when someone was either too bored with the station they had been given in my court or when they were too scared to truly gaze upon my face. Smile or no. Horrific or mollified for these . . . *humans*.

"We have art therap—"

"—what is your name?"

Clarity returned to his gaze and he swallowed, his Adam's apple bobbing. "My—My name, Your Majesty?"

I forced the smile to remain. I forced my true nature inside this pathetic cage and played pretend with him. "Did I stutter, young man?"

"N-No, of course not, Your Majesty."

"Good, because you do enough stuttering for the both of us." I touched the handle of my brush, never letting my attention leave his eyes as I waited for my answer.

But he did not offer it.

And I had lost my patience. "Are you going to make me repeat myself?!" My voice echoed off the mirror. The glass shattered, spilling pieces across my vanity. A dozen sliced into my hand and arm, causing tiny droplets of blood to well and dribble down onto the fine wood.

"I—Well, I—" This time, the man broke eye contact. He glanced over his shoulder, towards the door, panic pulsing through his veins loud enough for me to hear. The sound made my heart skip a beat in delight.

"So you will disregard a direct question *and* make me repeat myself?!"

He turned, the clipboard returning to his side, and strode towards the door. "Nurse! Grab the—"

"Do *not* walk away from me!" The room shook. The chandelier swung, and the pictures banged against the walls. The floor wobbled and swayed, throwing the man to the ground. His clipboard clattered away.

In that moment, my mirror played tricks on me. It showed him shouting toward the door, controlled determination furrowing his eyebrows as he called out about some patient. But when I whipped around, looking at him without the mirror, he lay curled in a ball and whimpering. "I was told not to tell you my name." His arms went over his head as my smile disappeared, taking the human façade with it.

I rose from my bench and strode across the room. My shadow dwarfed him. And the very sight caused me to chuckle. "Pathetic. Truly pathetic." My eyes flashed to the open door, knowing it to be nothing but an illusion. "Is this the best you can do?! Is this all you have?!"

Despite my screams, no one answered. No one responded, and I grew tired of the sniveling coward they'd sent to supplicate me today. The one they'd done such a lousy job training. It would honestly be a service to put him out of their misery . . . but I was not in the habit of doing my captors favors.

Besides, it's more fun being unpredictable.

Hints
M.R. Gavin

Tess wrapped her hands around the mug, lifting it to her lips. She had breathed in the smell of coffee for months, longing for a sip, but she no longer wanted it. She set it on the table, shifted her gaze to the window and wiped her eyes.

"How's your coffee? I added extra foam," Nate asked.

"It's great," Tess answered feigning a sip, "I don't know if coffee is going to be enough to survive Claire's birthday party."

"You can always have a beer. Plus, I'll be there."

"I can't handle their hints anymore" she explained.

"It's what family does," Nate answered, "They meddle."

"They don't know how much it hurts."

"They aren't trying to hurt you."

"But they are," Tess snapped, "I know they're family, but why can't they mind their own business?"

Nate got up, set his mug in the sink, and leaned against the counter.

"It's Trinity's day. Claire's first birthday is a big deal. Hopefully, they'll focus on that."

"Maybe," Tess replied without enthusiasm.

Tess and Nate were like most young adults with their own lives and friends away from their parents. They kept busy and enjoyed their independence but attended family functions almost monthly. Tess was tired of the conversations, the hints, the gossip, the expectations, and the guilt overshadowing every trip.

She brushed her hair, preparing herself for the deluge of comments she would get.

"Just smile and nod your head. Or go find Nate. Or play with Claire. Or hide," she muttered passing their mirror as she dressed for the party. She looked normal, her body mostly unchanged since college. She turned sideways and imagined, squeezing back the tears.

At one o'clock Claire's first birthday party began. Claire was their first niece and would be a big sister by the time she was two. Aunts, uncles, first cousins, second cousins, great aunts and uncles, grandparents and great-grandparents all arrived to celebrate. Tess flew under the radar, praying Nate was right, and there would be no hints, but it was early, and everyone was sober.

When they brought out the cake, Claire was wide-eyed but looked ready to use the cake as a pillow. The family sang "Happy Birthday," while Trinity and her husband encouraged Claire to blow out the candles. Claire slammed her fists into the cake, splattering the trio with icing.

151

"I hope someone recorded that," Tess said to Nate.

"Don't you two want one?!" Came a loud voice from behind them. Tess froze. Nate turned and chuckled, "Someday, but we still like to eat our cake."

Tess's reprieve was over. The aunt who made the comment wasn't a usual offender. Dad asked for Nate, leaving Tess trapped in the kitchen with aunts and cousins clucking over Claire, her cuteness, and her impending big sister title.

"Trinity is a natural mom," Aunt Mags said.

"Oh, yes, but all mothers are naturals. There is nothing to worry about," Francis said, glancing at Tess.

"And children bring so much joy! Did you see how adorable they were? Cake everywhere!" Aunt Erin added.

The room chortled as a pot of coffee was passed. Tess refused a cup.

"No coffee, Tess! Do you have something to tell us?" Mags winked.

Tess maintained her composure, "I already have a beer."

The women let out a synchronized sigh.

"You are planning on having children?"

"You're so good with the little ones!"

"I bet you are very maternal toward your students."

"You better start soon!"

Another round of laughter.

Aunt Mags leaned in, "Given how both families are so Catholic, we expected a pregnancy announcement right after the wedding."

Tess took a swig of beer.

"You'll have the cutest children!"

"I'd like to be an aunt," Trinity added.

Another gulp of beer, "I'm out of beer, excuse me." Tess shook with rage as she escaped to the yard feeling like a shell cracked by her family's hurtful words. Another beer might numb the pain.

She entered the garage prepared to confront the men of the family, get her beer, and find a place to hide.

"Tess!" Dad announced with a smile, "What can I get you?"

"Lager, please."

Nate opened her bottle. As she left, Uncle Max cried, "Stay a while, Tess!"

She sighed but stood next to Nate. The men returned to their renovation discussion.

"I wish Nate had been around to install the washer," Dad chuckled.

"Isn't it great to have your kids help?" Uncle George said.

"And to give you grandkids!" Uncle Max interjected, "Nothing's better than being a grandfather. Joe, don't you love having Claire?"

"Sure, I'd love a grandson too," he winked at Tess.

She balled her fists.

"Who knows what Trinity's having? Could be a boy," Nate answered redirecting the conversation.

"Oh, but they'll need cousins," George said, "You and your cousins were inseparable."

Everyone looked at Tess and Nate.

She was about to burst, when Nate spoke up, "Remember when we got stuck in your loft?"

And they flew down memory lane. Tess squeezed Nate with gratitude and snuck away to hide in the guest room. Her chest heaved, but she had no tears left. She wanted her family to know how their words stabbed the hollow place in her lower abdomen, but they were family. Family is unintentionally cruel. She wanted them to know with every hint, she remembered the past twenty-four months of praying. She thought about the three times she was late, convinced it had finally worked, only to be destroyed when her period arrived the next day. Eliminating her caffeine intake, abstaining from alcohol, so nothing would harm the baby they wanted. Finally, two months ago her period was late. She didn't want to hope, but when the days passed to a week, she bought a test. It was positive. They were finally going to have a baby. Nate beamed; Tess glowed. The next month was bliss despite the nausea and headaches. A week ago, she was eight weeks pregnant. Nate went with her to see the baby's heartbeat.

They didn't.

Every time she saw a child, she thought of this, but children she could handle. When they asked if she was a mommy yet, they wanted to feel safe, to tell her she'd be a good mommy, to ask her to be their mommy. Adults hint openly, harshly. They judge everything but never ask directly. That would be too far, but hinting doesn't hurt anyone. Hinting can only push them in the right direction.

Their hints magnified her feelings of emptiness, making her feel wasted and useless. She had survived the birthday party, but not without reopening wounds that had yet to heal.

Evenings with Ms. Lynn
K. T. Rose

Wade had to admit, the package gave him a hard time. Not only was it hard to find, it didn't go so willingly either. The package, or Bill as they called him in English, threw all two-hundred fifty pounds of himself around, planting blow after blow to Wade's face and chest, leaving scrapes, bruises, and broken bones. But it was nothing a bullet to the kneecap and the butt of the pistol to the back of the head couldn't handle.

Now we both have to show up to the party with broken noses. Nice going, asshole.

Though Bill was unconscious when the men came to pick them up, they felt the need to chloroform him anyway.

Showoffs, Wade thought as he slid into the passenger seat. Leather rubbing against Kevlar, he flicked his eyes as blood rushed down his throat and over his lips.

"You wanna clean that?" Asked the driver, his squinted eyes gleaming in the night lights as he smirked.

Wade scoffed and peered out the passenger window. The street was wide awake. Small men on bikes pedaled fast, veering in and out of traffic. The drunk and possibly homeless limped through the streets slurring Yen through missing teeth. Short women in sheer dresses huddled together, giggling and pointing at places of interest. Clubs banged electronica. Bars swelled to capacity.

This block was a good place to go missing.

The driver chuckled. "I see you're not much of a talker still, huh?"

Wade ran his fingers through his short dark hair before flexing his broad shoulders. If he had a penny for every time he'd been asked that, he'd lost count ten years ago. Aside from avoiding petty small talk, being an international hitman had its perks, like traveling the world with a seemingly bottomless expense account. Getting into a tussle here and there wasn't all bad especially in the current instance. Japan was one of his favorite places and Ms. Lynn was one of his favorite clients.

Since the twenty-something took over as commander-in-chief of her family's 'association' when her father got his brains blown out by a rival a few years ago, Ms. Lynn had to be more than assertive to the dangerous men who followed her.

She'd set examples for them, pushing their uncertainties in her favor as they were forced to witness her decapitating or cutting the heart out of those considered disloyal. Since she wasn't sure who she could trust among her men, she'd hire Wade to go find those who've gone rogue, deliver them, and enjoy the show. Though it was simple, Wade was sure his attendance to the show had a double meaning. Her shallow message had to be conveyed to all.

But who could blame her? Knowing that she could be assassinated by any of her soldiers or rivals had to be nerve wrecking. Wade could care less about her wellbeing, status, reasons, or whatever point she wanted to portray though. He only cared about executing the job and of course, the pay.

Ms. Lynn was waiting patiently on the vacant fifth floor of one of the office buildings on her family's shipyard. The booming of heavy machinery, men yelling and the bellowing of ship horns riddled the night along with the unforgiving stitch of rotted fish and salt water. Each wall of the dank, abandoned fifth floor was packed with several men and one of them (*a teenager?*) held the familiar Katana sword. Its aqua wooden sheath was embroidered throughout with a silhouette of a thin, golden dragon. He held it with open hands as if it were being Christened.

Wade chuckled to himself. Although the Katana was Ms. Lynn's preferred method of execution, she kept a 9mm pistol in her leather hip holster. Wade chalked it up to her being prepared for whatever fight was to come, just as any good leader would.

In the center of the dim floor was a steel chair backed by a child-sized steel bucket full of water, a hand towel and a medium sized cooking pot.

That's new.

Wade and one of Ms. Lynn's men tied unconscious Bill to the steel chair, bounding each leg and his torso with hemp rope. His arms were tied behind the backing of the chair.

"Wade," Ms. Lynn said softly as she approached him. Her sweet voice was as graceful as a songbirds as her long dark hair flowed behind her with every step. She floated with the femininity of a beautiful geisha ready to place a healing hand on a weary soldier's lap. However, her dark eyes told the story of a power-drunken Komodo with a belly full of fire that was ready to vomit.

"Ms. Lynn," Wade said with a nod.

"Didn't look too easy for you this time," she said, using her small index finger to motion at her button nose.

"You know me, I prefer challenges." Wade had forgotten about his deformed nose, one nostril stuffed with gauze. Aside from the occasional stinging, he had grown used to it.

"Well I'm happy you got your challenge, but the night is still young," she said as she removed her leather jacket, exposing the tattoos of dragons and goat heads that consumed her upper back and forearms.

Her army boots and a black tank top made her war- ready. She removed a pink hair band from one of the many pockets of her cargo pants and tied her hair into a bun, sitting it atop her perfectly round head.

"Wade," she began, "do you know what *waterboarding* is?"

Of course, he did. His brief stint as a CIA spy rewarded him with the misfortune of being on the wrong side of the assault. *That's what I got for talking so much shit*, he thought but said, "I'm familiar."

155

"*Bill* has information that I want. You will waterboard him with the help from my men until he gives it up."

Wade nodded.

Bill shifted his head, coming out of his induced coma, then he started to shake his wrist behind him. The easy, passive movement became violent when he peered up at Ms. Lynn. He pulled limbs away from the chair and against the rope, slicing his flesh against the hemp fibers.

You're not going anywhere, buddy, Wade thought as he watched almost elated that the bastard's face was soaking in fear.

"Didn't think I would find you, huh?" Ms. Lynn asked. "I knew you wouldn't get far."

Bill shifted from left to right, taking the chair down to the floor onto its side. The *thud* of Bill slamming to the floor was accompanied by a *crack* as he landed on his left arm. His scream echoed out, swallowing up the noise from the dock.

"Looks like you broke something," Ms. Lynn said, kicking at Bill's arm as it lay wedged underneath him. Bill shrieked as she motioned for one of her men to flip him onto his back. He let out another agonizing cry as all his weight came down on his broken arm and hands that were now against the grimy cement floor.

"Why'd you steal from me?" she asked as Bill screamed and grimaced. Wade smirked as he admired her stance over the huge crying man and the attention she had from the sea of dangerous men who crowded the space, standing against the walls engaged in silence.

"Why'd you steal from me, Bill?" she asked again.

Bill began screaming Yen when Ms. Lynn interrupted, "English only, please. We don't want to be rude to our guest."

Obviously, Bill didn't care because he continued yelling in their native tongue. Ms. Lynn turned to one of her men and nodded. He and another man lifted the chair and sat Bill up right. They leaned the chair on its two back legs, positioning his head over the bucket.

Ms. Lynn turned to Wade and, with a vacant face, nodded.

Wade placed the wet towel over Bill's face and poured water from the pot onto it. Bill choked and coughed as he shook his head trying to avoid the steady stream, but was powerless. After a few seconds, the men dropped Bill back to the floor. He choked and gagged and screamed all at once as his weight crushed his hands underneath him. Wade was sure the man's hands had been reduced to mush by now.

Finally, Bill screamed out in broken English, "I give it back! I give—it back! Hasyu—has it! My brother Hasyu—is hiding it! Please! Please! I go get it! I bring it back! Please—" He choked up spit and sucked in air.

Well, that was easy, Wade thought as he stepped back from the puddle around Bill's head.

Ms. Lynn grinned as she reached into the top pocket on her left thigh. She pulled a gold necklace that was anchored by a quarter-sized sapphire gem. "Not anymore."

Bill's eyes widened as she laughed maniacally and motioned at one of the men near the staircase. The man left for a minute or two. On his return, the men clear the way as he dragged a body that had a bloody stump where a head used to be and dropped it in front of Bill.

The body was wearing a baby blue t-shirt with the Dragon Ball Z logo across the front. Its jeans were dyed burgundy by blood. Its stump was a mess of what looked like blood-stained noodles intertwined with a thick white bone.

"Hasyu!" Bill screamed. "Why?"

"Because I can," Ms. Lynn spat, glaring at the faces around the floor, including Wade's. "Sit him up," she demanded as she motioned for the boy who was holding the samurai sword to come forward. He did. After the men sat the chair upright, she pulled the sword from the wooden scabbard while glaring at Bill who was whimpering as he dripped water and spit from his face. His eyes hadn't moved from his brother's lifeless body.

The sword tore through the air and sliced through Bill's thick neck effortlessly. His head popped off and rolled across the floor toward a cluster of men, who dared not move or speak. Just watched. Thick crimson liquid spewed up and out, stunned by the circulatory disruption.

Ms. Lynn returned the sword to its sheath and searched the room once more. Her dead eyes brought down that icy hot sensation Wade got when he felt someone tailing him as she sent out a cynical message to all that stood before her.

Once her eyes landed on Wade, she said "Let's clean you up, get you paid and get some dinner. I'm starving." She smiled.

Wade nodded. This was his favorite part about Japan: spending the evening with a dangerously powerful, sex-crazed Japanese woman who was paying him a million dollars.

He smiled and followed her to the exit, leaving the men to clean up the mess.

Note to the Reader

We hope you enjoyed our publication! If you have, we ask that you please consider writing a brief review for the book on Amazon.com. In your review, be sure to mention the title of the writing (or the name of the author) that you enjoyed the most—we will take reader reviews heavily into account when it comes time to decide who will receive our first solo-author book deals later this year!

About Z Publishing House

Begun as a blog in the fall of 2015, Z Publishing, LLC, has since transitioned into book publishing. This transition is in response to the problem plaguing the publishing world: For writers, finding new readers can be tremendously difficult, and for readers, finding new, talented authors with whom they identify is like finding a needle in a haystack. With Z Publishing, no longer will anyone will anyone have to go about this process alone. By producing anthologies of multiple authors rather than single-author volumes, Z Publishing hopes to harbor a community of readers and writers, bringing all sides of the industry closer together.

To sign up for the Z Publishing newsletter or to submit your own writing to a future anthology, visit www.zpublishinghouse.com. You can also follow the evolution of Z Publishing on the following platforms:

Facebook: www.facebook.com/zpublishing
Twitter: www.twitter.com/z_publishing

Author Biographies

Allison Astorino: Allison Astorino is the author of the novel *A Place to Stand*, which is currently available on Amazon. She resides in Michigan, where she works at a small urban farm in the metro Detroit area. She recently graduated with a degree in English literature from the University of Michigan and hopes to continue her education in creative writing. A variety of her short stories have been published in the on campus literary journal *Lyceum*.

Halley Bass: Halley is a young writer and musician from Ann Arbor, Michigan. She has had work published in the *Huron River Review*, Washtenaw Community College's award-winning literary magazine.

Heidi Ann Barson: Heidi was raised in Detroit, Michigan. She finds her passion in writing many genres. Sometimes whimsical, other times dark, and often philosophical, she attempts to capture the reader's heartfelt emotion. She works by day and writes by night, always keeping her passion alive!

Renée Beaudoin: Born and raised in Michigan, Renée Beaudoin graduated from Western Michigan University with a bachelor's degree in English: creative writing. Working retail by day and freelance writing by night, she fills the few remaining hours learning how to draw.

Melanie Noell Bernard: Melanie Noell Bernard hails from the Midwest. Surrounded by endless fog and bitter winter nights, she quickly fell in love with the dark. Combine that with a knack for the gritty, the disturbing, and the creepy, you have the beginnings of a horror writer.

Leah Blaetterlein: Leah Blaetterlein is a senior at the University of Michigan–Dearborn studying English and communications. She is an active staff member for the *Lyceum*, the university's literary journal. Three of her pieces have also been published in the journal. She thanks her family and friends for their continued support.

M. Andrew Bodinger: Andy currently teaches ESL in China. Beyond that, he enjoys thinking about narratives in all forms of media, forgetting and rediscovering the benefits of exercise, and reminiscing about hummus and black beans. Andy graduated from Western Michigan University in 2016.

Nathan Calkin: Nathan was born and raised in Michigan. He attended the University of Detroit Mercy, where he received his degree in psychology and a minor in creative writing.

Benjamin Champagne: Benjamin Champagne is co-owner and director of Counter Culture Arts Collective in Saginaw, Michigan. He helps with music, art, and just about every type of production. He works in interstitial mediums of art, from writing to music and film collage. He has one of those motivational posters on his wall.

A.C. Crider: A.C. wrote his first novel at eighteen. It was a complete disaster, but since then he's published a few short stories. At thirty-two, with more skill, he is back to work on a new book. A.C. lives on the shores of Lake Michigan in the tourist trap town of South Haven in southwest Michigan with his wife and three children.

Brandin Dahlstrom: Brandin is thrilled to be back in the creative world. He hopes to showcase his work here and in the future in both fiction and comedy.

Anna Dunigan: Anna Dunigan is a student at Grand Valley State University. She started writing in elementary school with a story about flying shoes and hasn't stopped since, though now her stories have a little more substance. She loves using her comedic style to make people smile.

Shane Emery: Shane Emery grew up and lives in southeast Michigan. He currently attends Eastern Michigan University, on track to graduate with a degree in English education in the fall of 2018. He has a particular interest in teaching for environmental justice in literature.

Luke Fortier: Luke was born in Grand Rapids, Michigan, where he will be graduating with an associate degree in sociology. For the past few years, he has been working to gain a greater understanding of the mental and community health in working and volunteering for mental health and substance abuse facilities and events in Grand Rapids. Writing has been a passion of his from a young age and he has pursued knowledge of writing and literature independently. He is considering a career in law but plans always to have a hand in writing.

M.R. Gavin: M.R. Gavin is a writer from metro Detroit who writes literary fiction, horror, fantasy, science fiction, and children's literature. Gavin enjoys reading and avoiding large social gatherings by finding the nearest dog. For more writing, visit www.mrgavin1991.wordpress.com.

Justin Gawel: Justin Gawel is a selfish man who lives in northern Michigan.

Michael V. Gibson: Michael V. Gibson is a writer and editor whose work frequently appears in the literary journals of several countries. In 2016, he founded *The Magnitizdat Literary*, an international journal of poetry and prose, and his first chapbook, *Hôtel Souvenir*, was published in 2017. A second, *Passengers*, is forthcoming.

Niikah Hatfield: Niikah Hatfield is currently a student at Northern Michigan University of Marquette, where she is studying ceramics and creative writing. When not creating stories or artwork, she is often outside, playing music, or chasing after dreams. She is the author of *Kana's Vardo* and her work is published in *Adelaide Review*, *Ore Ink Review*, *404 Words*, and others.

Esther Haven: Esther Haven now lives in a small Ohio town with her cat, KJ, the little black panther. Her heart, however, is still back in Michigan, where she was born and raised. Esther studied creative writing throughout her undergraduate studies and dreams of publishing a novel one day.

Wade Holcomb: Wade Holcomb is an amateur writer, musician, and photographer in Lansing, Michigan. When not writing, he spends his time being a law student at Michigan State University.

Dan Jones: Dan Jones self-published his psychological thriller *Crystal and Her Family* and has written, produced, and directed three full-length feature films, including the award-winning *Human Achievement*. He continues to write while attaining his license as a clinical therapist. Dan's plan: assist and entertain.

Grant Kammer: Grant Kammer is a recent graduate of Aquinas College. A lifelong resident of Michigan, Grant is currently based in Grand Rapids, working at a nonprofit and doing freelance writing. His short fiction and creative nonfiction have been previously published in the *Aquinas College Sampler*, and his journalism can be found through Rapid Growth Media.

Sarah A. Kenney: Sarah A. Kenney is a Michigan-based author, also known as the Cursed Author. From the age of twelve years old, she has been writing her nightmares down and turning them into stories ranging from YA fantasy to adult psychological thrillers. Sarah began publishing her works on Amazon in 2016. These include her YA fantasy series (*The Devils Curse Novels*), adult psychological series (*The Keyhole Novels*), and three chapbooks—*What Dreams are Made of . . .*, *Carousel*, and newly released, *Corrupted Minds*. Her next series will be released in September: *The Eternal Enemies Series*. You can find her weekly chapter writing of adult crime-thriller, *Heads or Tails*, on Wattpad.

Chris Lawitzke: Chris Lawitzke lives in Grand Rapids, Michigan. He is a recent graduate of Grand Valley State University. You can review more of his writings at www.clawitzke.wordpress.com.

Delia Lee: Delia Lee was an everyday science student until the day she was forced to write a short fiction story. That day in creative writing class is something she never regrets. She currently lives in a state that is her muse and encourages her to see life through a different lens.

Megan Locatis: Megan Locatis is a Midwestern writer with a penchant for all things sci-fi, horror, and fantasy. She has a soft spot in her heart for dystopian fiction and is currently working on her first sci-fi novel.

Amanda Lott: Amanda is a graduate of the University of Michigan, with a degree in journalism and screen studies. However, she's been a writer her whole life. She currently lives in Dearborn and works at the home of several published and unpublished writers—Starbucks.

T. A. Majeski: T. A. Majeski lives and writes in Michigan, where she tutors English at a community college and restrains her wanderlust.

Cullen E McCurdy: Cullen McCurdy currently lives in Holt, Michigan, with a bachelor's in creative writing. He primarily writes high fantasy and science fiction and keeps his writer's blog at www.northbornswordsman.blog.

Bryce Meerhaeghe: Bryce is a psychology researcher from the great state of Michigan, currently living in North Carolina. He misses snow.

Eli T. Mond: Eli T. Mond is the pen name of David Davis, a writer and artist from Detroit, Michigan. He is the founding editor of *Hyperlimenous* (a.k.a. the *Ibis Head Review*), a contemporary art and culture webzine, and has had work published in various journals. He can be found online at www.elitmond.com.

Kyle Mykietiuk: Kyle Mykietiuk is a student at the University of Michigan working toward a degree in philosophy. Kyle lives in Flint, Michigan.

Gabi O.: Gabi is an amateur photographer and college student from Michigan. Her own love of reading inspired her to try her hand at writing, and she's currently drafting a novel, or three. She has two guinea pigs and too many houseplants.

Giulia Genevieve Pink: Giulia Pink is a professional tarot reader, copywriter, and freelance illustrator from Detroit. She enjoys cups of tea, cuddling her cats, and reading gothic fiction. She recently left the corporate world to start a small tarot and writing business.

Brennan Quenneville: Brennan Quenneville is a writer living in Michigan. He is a contributor at the *Read Option* and *Type in Stereo* and can be found at his personal blog, www.brennquenn.com.

Kelli Rajala: Kelli Rajala is a twenty-five-year-old residing in Marquette, Michigan. She's lived in the Upper Peninsula her entire life and often uses the frigid, northern winters as inspiration for her writing. In her free time, she's either writing, reading, painting, or designing jewelry.

Andrew Ronzino: From a young age, Andrew Ronzino has enjoyed reading and writing. For the joy of challenging himself, he participates in National Novel Writing Month (NaNoWriMo) every year and uses it to try new writing skills, genres, and styles. He lives in Grandville, Michigan.

K. T. Rose: K. T. Rose is a horror, thriller, and dark fiction writer from Detroit. She posts suspense and horror flash fiction on her blog at www.kyrobooks.com and is the author of a gruesome, suspenseful short story series titled *A Trinity of Wicked Tales* and an erotic thriller novel titled *When We Swing—An Erotic Thriller.*

Jared Sebastian: Jared Sebastian was born and raised in southeast Michigan and graduated from Western Michigan University with a BA in creative writing. He can usually be found writing, reading, or stressing about the fact that he is not writing enough. Jared can be contacted at sebastian_jared@yahoo.com.

Ranyas Senestela: Ranyas Senestela has been writing for sixteen years, enjoying favorite books such as *The Lord of the Rings, The Hobbit, Harry Potter,* and *A Song of Ice and Fire.* Ranyas enjoys many genres but prefers science fiction, fantasy, and historical fiction. Some of her favorite works are by Philippa Greggory, Anne Rice, and Ken Follett. Normally, Ranyas enjoys writing and reading, but when she isn't on adventures, she's tending to creative pursuits like sculpture and painting. Ranyas is a proud Ravenclaw and an adamant participant in National Novel Writing Month. She has also been published on a Japanese-based website called *MyAnimeList* and is a big fan of *Naruto, Code Geass,* and *Soul Eater.*

Sarah Sorensen: Sarah Sorensen has been published over forty times in small presses. She is currently at work on her first novel. Find her at www.typefingertapdancer.wordpress.com or buy her a coffee in Kalamazoo, Michigan.

Andrea Stepchuk: Andrea Stepchuk graduated from the University of Michigan–Dearborn with a business marketing degree. She currently works full-time as a sales support specialist in the Detroit area. She enjoys crocheting and spending time with her husband, family, and friends.

Moya Tobey: Moya Tobey is a college student in Michigan who spends her days doing homework, reading books, and living in worlds far from her own. She has a passion for God and enjoys spreading the love of Christ on a daily basis.

Madison Vassari: Madison Vassari originally hails from Findlay, Ohio, and is a graduate of Ohio University. He is presently channeling his inner Steinbeck as he travels in search of America while cataloguing his experience on his website, www.likecaine.com.

Breezy White: Breezy White is an old soul with a young will to explore. She devours books to no end, is a self-professed nap junkie, adores poetry, and needs the color black.

Made in the USA
Columbia, SC
12 September 2018